D1014962

Prayer    Greatest    fruits    Duties
     (Privilege)    of
              (Spirit)

Page 21 – 38 – 40    80

Speak            faginness

101    102      108-109

# FACING YOUR FEELINGS

*Moving from Emotional Bondage
to Spiritual Freedom*

by
Vickie Kraft

WORD PUBLISHING
Dallas·London·Vancouver·Melbourne

Facing Your Feelings
Moving from Emotional Bondage to Spiritual Freedom
by Vickie Kraft

Unless otherwise indicated, Scripture quotations used in this book are from the Holy Bible, New International Version (NIV). Copyright © 1973, 1978, 1984 International Bible Society. Used by permission of Zondervan Bible Publishers.

Scripture references indicated KJV are from the King James Version of the Bible.

References indicated NKJV are from the New King James Version. Copyright © 1979, 1980, 1982, 1992, Thomas Nelson, Inc., Publisher.

Incidents, anecdotes, and case histories described in this volume are based on actual cases; however names and other details have been changed, if necessary, to protect the identities. Some anecdotes are composites of several cases.

Amy Carmichael's poem, "Thou Art My Lord Who Slept Upon a Pillow," from *Edges of His Ways*, copyright 1955, is used by permission of the Dohnavur Fellowship, England, and the Christian Literature Crusade, Fort Washington, Pennsylvania.

ISBN 0-8499-3857-0 (tpw)

*Printed in the United States of America.*

*To my daughters,*

*Helene, Alison, and Gaylan,*

*and my granddaughters,*

*Adrian and Alexandra.*

OTHER BOOKS BY VICKIE KRAFT:

*The Influential Woman (Word)*

*Women Mentoring Women (Moody)*

# Contents

# Acknowledgments

I'M GRATEFUL FOR THE RESPONSE of the hundreds of women who heard this material taught in weekly Bible lessons. They assured me that the Lord was meeting their needs as they studied men and women of the Bible and identified with their human weaknesses and their dependence on God.

I'm also indebted to Nancy Norris, my editor at Word Publishing and my friend, who encouraged me to put these lessons into a book. She has carefully guided each step of the process, and I'm grateful for her professional skill.

Lela Gilbert has my appreciation for her contribution and careful editing. I'm also grateful for the discernment and help Sue Ann Jones has shown in copyediting.

*Vickie Kraft*

$\mathcal{S}$O WHAT IS YOUR GUT REACTION? Tell me how you *really* feel."

"It's a perfect match—they're madly in love, and she has nothing but good feelings about him."

"Let's go for it! My sense is that we're doing the right thing."

These familiar sound bytes indicate that our modern world is deeply sensitive to human emotions. In fact, more often than not, our feelings are our compass, guiding our decision-making process. We call it "following our hearts instead of our heads." Of course, we know that emotions are a God-given part of our lives, allowing us to vividly experience the world. But as Christian women, we have to ask ourselves if emotional satisfaction should be our primary goal in life.

The answer is clearly *no*.

The evidence around us suggests that modern emotions are creating subjective standards that aren't the least bit trustworthy. Broken marriages, abused children, and teenage suicides proclaim out-of-control emotions. *Wants* that are falsely identified as *needs* keep family credit cards maxed out and finances in shambles. And "if it feels good, do it" was a deadly motto for thousands of people now suffering from sexually transmitted diseases.

My years as a wife, mother, and Bible teacher have taught me that God's Word provides an *objective* set of standards for daily living. Naturally, these standards don't always "feel good" when we first confront them. For example, when God calls upon us to treat others the way we'd like to be treated ourselves, personal sacrifice is necessary. When He requires us to obey His commandments, doing so may conflict with our deepest cravings. Most disturbing of all, He firmly challenges us to set all else aside when we submit ourselves to His sovereign will.

On a day-to-day basis, we are faced with hundreds of choices, thousands of challenges, and countless temptations. In the pages that follow, we'll reflect upon the emotional experiences of both contemporary women and historic men and women who lived in biblical times. I hope our inquiry into their lives will encourage you to bring your will into line with the biblical principles we'll study. Once you've made a willful decision to choose God's way, you'll find that your *emotions* will follow. When women do this, I can tell you the results are life changing.

Why is dealing with our emotions—facing our feelings—so important? While positive emotions add luster to life, negative emotions can be very damaging. If we ignore them, become obsessed with them, or refuse to confront them, they will stunt our spiritual growth. The truth is, we cannot be *spiritually* mature unless we are *emotionally* mature. My prayer is that, with the help of the Holy Spirit, this book will enlighten and inspire you toward emotional health and its inevitable result—spiritual growth.

# 1

## Nurturing Our Spiritual and Emotional Growth

**W**HEN GOD CREATED US in His image, that image included our emotions. God gives us all things to enjoy, and healthy emotions bring color and zest to our lives. His Word says, "God . . . richly provides us with everything for our enjoyment" (1 Tim. 6:17). We're also told in Scripture to enjoy our work, our mates, our children, our good health, our material blessings, and our God. Without emotions, that would be impossible.

We *enjoy* God. We *enjoy* our families and our friends. We *enjoy* the opportunities God gives us to use our abilities to serve others. Life has purpose and fulfillment. Our spiritual life matures and deepens as we appreciate God's blessings.

When everything is working out—when we move into a new home, when our children finish college and find a good job, when they marry the right woman or man, when we have a good report from the doctor, when we actually have money left over at the end of the month—these occurrences make us happy. Our emotions respond and react to our physical circumstances.

Our emotions also react to our *spiritual* circumstances. When a person, overwhelmed with guilt, finds forgiveness by trusting in Jesus Christ, he or she feels cleansed and free. We often see this happen in women who have carried the guilt and pain of abortion for years; they tell us they have found emotional and spiritual healing through Christ's forgiveness, particularly within the context of a support group for abortion recovery. After immorality has destroyed their self-worth, I've seen women renounce their unhealthy lifestyles and find joy in obedience to the Lord.

But what if our emotions become a runaway train we can't control? Perhaps you often feel overwhelmed by your emotions and you see yourself in the following descriptions:

- Have you experienced rejection or been treated unfairly, or are you struggling with emotional devastation from the past—were you molested or neglected?
- Are you in a marriage that has soured and you feel hopeless?
- Do others say you seem to "have it all together," but underneath the surface you are seething with anger and bitterness, unable to forgive things that were done to you?
- Are you overwhelmed with guilt and regret for things you have done and you just can't forgive yourself?

When we face uncertain, painful, or tragic circumstances in life, we feel sorrow, confusion, anger, and pain. These emotions are also God-given; our Father uses these feelings to push us closer to Him. Just as physical pain tells us something is wrong with our bodies, so emotional pain may be

God's way of telling us all is not well with our spiritual relationship with Him.[1]

When emotions become destructive, they can make us miserable, ruin our relationships with others, and stunt our spiritual growth. They build a solid wall between us and God, and between us and other people.

In our misery, we can't help but feel that God is somehow to blame for the tragic events of our past or the unhappiness of our present, and it's hard for us to trust a God who allows such tragedy to happen to His children. So we keep our distance from Him. We do just enough to keep our membership in His "club," but there's no sense of connection, no real enjoyment of God's presence, and not a lot of honest fellowship with other believers.

In the pages ahead, we'll see how these untempered, destructive emotions—selfishness, guilt, fear, worry, inability to forgive, anger, envy, rejection, greed, pride, feelings of inferiority, disappointment, discontentment, grief, and loneliness—can hinder our spiritual growth and keep us from having a close, trusting relationship with our Creator. By studying biblical characters who also endured these emotions and by applying God's holy Word, we'll also see how we can face these feelings, overcome these emotional obstacles, and proceed with strength and courage on the walk the Lord planned for us. And in the end, we'll gain a new appreciation for friendship and see how Christian friends can stimulate each other's emotional growth and emotional maturity.

Maybe you're thinking no one could ever understand the misery your emotions have led you to feel right now. Maybe you secretly think your situation is past healing. If so, please remember what the prophet Jeremiah prayed as he watched his world crumble before his eyes: "Ah, Sovereign LORD, you have made the heavens and the earth by your great power and outstretched arm. *Nothing is too hard for you"* (Jer. 32:17 emphasis mine).

God's clearly stated purpose for all of His children is that we grow into spiritual maturity. He can take us around, over, or through any obstacle that has retarded our spiritual growth. Nothing from our past or in our present is too hard for Him to handle. God created our emotions, and He is able to stop their destructive effect on our lives. He can make our emotions work for us, giving us peace and joy as we learn to respond to our relationship with our Lord rather than react to our circumstances.

The task may seem great, but with God's help it's really not all that hard. In this book, we'll work through the challenge together, and by the time you've reached the epilogue, I hope you'll be well on your way to dealing effectively with any emotional obstacles that block your progress toward spiritual maturity. But here in the beginning, we'll "start small," moving toward the goal of spiritual maturity with baby steps . . .

## Measuring Spiritual Growth

To our great delight, our granddaughter Adrian visited us recently. Nearly a year ago when she was staying in our home, my husband had marked her height and the date on the doorframe in the kitchen. Leading her to that same mark on the doorway, I smiled at her and said, "Let's see how tall you are now!"

She stood straight and tall as I marked the molding with a pencil point, level with the top of her head. She had grown three inches! I hugged her and told her how wonderful it was that she was getting so big.

Meanwhile, our family has joyfully welcomed another baby. When my daughter Helene gave birth to Alexandra, we held the newborn in our arms and loved her lavishly. Although little Alexandra was a tiny baby, she was fully human. Nothing will ever be added to make her more so. At birth, all the potential of her life was wrapped up in a seven-pound-three-ounce bundle.

When Alexandra came home from the hospital, nothing was expected of her. Her parents took full responsibility for her. Mother's milk was her only source of physical nourishment, and for the first few months, Helene's entire life revolved around the needs of her infant daughter. As weeks went by, we saw the baby filling out, following us with her eyes, smiling real smiles. She was changing and maturing.

Both Adrian and Alexandra are growing, but there's a big difference in our expectations for each of them. Adrian is three years older. She can talk and understand. She knows what it means to obey and to disobey. She knows why she is being disciplined. She can eat by herself and dress herself. Alexandra will have a lot of growing to do before she catches up with Adrian. We love both the children equally, but each one is at a different level of growth.

There is an exact parallel between physical growth and spiritual growth—except perhaps that spiritual growth is less measurable. Spiritual growth cannot be demonstrated by marks on a doorframe. Still, there are many similarities. When we come to know Jesus Christ as our Savior, we receive a new nature, and we become God's children—spiritual infants. All the potential for our spiritual life is given to us at the moment we trust Christ, because the Holy Spirit comes to live within us, never to leave us.

## Knowing God's Word

But that is only the beginning. From that time on, we are intended to mature in our spiritual lives. And the first food we need is milk: "Like newborn babies, crave pure spiritual milk, so that by it you may grow up in your salvation, now that you tasted that the Lord is good" (1 Pet. 2:2).

We initially taste the goodness of the Lord when we realize He will forgive our sins and make us His children. We come to understand that He does these things, not because of anything good we have done, but solely because of His mercy and grace toward us. He loves us so much He came to earth Himself as a human being and took the punishment we deserve for our sins. Therefore, when we receive God's gift of eternal life through Jesus Christ, we taste God's goodness.

But we are babies, and we need spiritual milk to grow. That milk is God's Word. We also need other essential "nutrients" to help us grow toward spiritual maturity. Those essentials are prayer, fellowship, and obedience.

When we say that God's Word is our "milk," we imply that someone must help us understand it and must feed it to us in a way that helps us assimilate it. We need nurturing and mentoring. Maybe you have not grown as you should have because you didn't have someone to help you when you were a spiritual baby. That happens more than it should. But it's not too late—you can still go on to spiritual maturity.

However, this "bottle-feeding" is not supposed to go on for a lifetime. As you grow in your understanding, you will become able to digest and assimilate the meat of God's Word on your own. You'll be able to study and apply the Scripture for yourself. God's goal for each of His children is maturity. Paul wrote, "Prepare God's people for works of service, so that the body of Christ may be built up until we all reach unity in the faith and in the knowledge of the Son of God and become mature, attaining to the whole measure of the fullness of Christ" (Eph. 4:12–13).

## Prayer to Our Father

God's Word is the first essential for spiritual growth. But, as I said earlier, there are other necessities as well. Just as a human baby needs her mother, she also needs intimacy with her father. As new believers, we develop that intimacy with our heavenly Father through prayer. In fact, He has given us a wonderful promise when we pray to Him: "Do not be anxious about anything, but in everything by prayer and petition, with thanksgiving, present your requests to God. And the peace of God, which transcends all understanding, will guard your hearts and your minds in Christ Jesus" (Phil. 4:6–7).

God doesn't ask us to pray because He doesn't know our needs. He knows everything! We don't pray for His sake, but for ours. How else can we experience the reality of His love unless we tell Him our heartaches, needs, longings, and joys? How else can we feel His comfort and see His answers?

Have you ever prayed about a situation and felt God's presence and peace even though nothing had changed? Praying makes us spend time with our Father. Prayer makes us depend on Him. Prayer strengthens our faith. Prayer is essential to our spiritual growth. But there's more.

## Fellowship with Other Believers

In addition to nourishing ourselves with God's Word and spending time in prayer, we also need the nourishment that comes from spending time with other believers. As

Paul wrote, "Let us consider how we may spur one another on toward love and good deeds. Let us not give up meeting together, as some are in the habit of doing, but let us encourage one another" (Heb. 10:24–25).

When Christians talk about *fellowship*, we don't simply mean attending church on Sunday morning. It isn't enough to hear the sermon and walk out with no connection to anyone. It's important to *plan into our schedules* regular times of meeting with other believers, to encourage and build each other up, to share love, laughter, pain, and sorrow.

I had lunch recently with a friend. We always enjoy being together, but this time we found that we were having similar problems in a particular relationship. We were able to express how confused we felt and how hurt. We were able to suggest an approach to each other that might work. After we parted, I had a great feeling of satisfaction and enjoyment. In fact, we both did. Just to be able to talk about things and encourage and challenge one another helped lift an emotional burden from each of us. Fellowship is vital to spiritual maturity. King Solomon wrote, "As iron sharpens iron, so one [person] sharpens another" (Prov. 27:27).

## Obedience to God's Word

Fellowship is essential to spiritual maturity, and so is spiritual exercise. Just as a little baby must use its arms and legs and lift its head up to make its muscles develop and become stronger, spiritual growth requires exercise too.

Think of how a child learns to walk. At first it can only take one or two steps at a time. Then gradually, as its muscles become stronger, the child can walk effortlessly for the rest of its life. As we exercise the muscles of obedience to

God's Word, we will find it easier to obey; sin loses its appeal, and our discernment increases. Scripture teaches us, "Anyone who lives on milk, being still an infant, is not acquainted with the teaching about righteousness. But solid food is for the mature, who by constant use have trained themselves to distinguish good from evil" (Heb. 5:13–14).

## Failure to Thrive

If it were possible to measure your spiritual growth, how much do you think it would indicate you have grown in the last year or five years or ten? Some of us never seem to get past the infant stage. We accepted Jesus Christ as our personal Savior years ago, but our lives haven't been transformed all that much. We do a lot of the right things, but we don't feel a great connection with God. We are not overflowing with joy the way we thought we would be. There's no excitement or adventure in our spiritual journey. It's all rather ho-hum.

You may be thinking, "I'm not very mature. I don't feel close to God. Even when I pray I don't really expect an answer. I'm going through the motions, but it's not working. When I'm with other Christians I feel like a hypocrite."

I believe this happens, at least in part, due to another condition that parallels what happens in some babies. It's called "failure to thrive," and I think it can be a spiritual condition as well as a physical problem.

What keeps us from thriving? What stunts our spiritual lives and frustrates our development? Why are we disappointed in the Christian life? Why does God seem far away, not intimate or near?

Sometimes this failure to thrive is caused by emotional obstacles that have crippled us, given us a wrong concept of God, or made us devalue our worth. When it comes to emotional health, there are two extremes we must avoid. The first is ignoring or denying our feelings. "Stuffing" emotions causes them to smolder beneath the surface and affect our entire personalities.

On the other hand, we can't make our feelings the focus of our attention, as society today seems to have done with the motto, "If it *feels* good, do it." Our world has denied moral absolutes and traditional values, and instead the prevailing attitude seems to advocate doing whatever we feel like.

There are many examples of this "feel-good" attitude. For one thing, sex is viewed as nothing but an animal instinct, divorced from the protective framework of marriage and devoid of intimacy and commitment. I don't have to draw a picture of the harvest we are reaping as a result!

Other examples are plentiful: Selfishness is applauded and encouraged. Men and women walk out of marriages. Children are aborted, neglected, abused, and often left to raise themselves. Aged parents are abandoned, sometimes left helpless and starving, because their needs intrude on the self-centeredness of their adult children. Uncontrolled anger is exploding in random violence unparalleled in our history as a nation. All of this and more are the results of blindly following our feelings without respecting God-given moral restraints.

## Principles of Emotional Health

Neither denial of our emotions nor blind obedience to them will result in well-developed personalities. We must go back to the Bible for some important facts and principles about how to handle our emotions in a godly manner,[2] beginning with the idea that:

*God has emotions and created us in His image with a similar emotional capacity.*

God loves, is joyful, feels compassion, sorrow, and anger. Jesus Christ, as a human being, revealed to us the heart of God. He expressed sorrow, anger, frustration (Luke 9:41), disappointment and amazement (Luke 7:9), grief (John 12:39), and joy (Heb. 12:2). Our emotional makeup is one of the ways God's image is seen in us.

Next, we need to remember:

*Human beings are physical, spiritual, and emotional unities.*

We relate to our environment with our bodies, and we relate to God through our spirits. Our emotions are affected by both relationships. We simply cannot separate the different components of our natures into watertight compartments. "Just as we are able to experience physical pain or pleasure, so we have the capacity to experience emotional pain or pleasure."[3]

## Emotions Powerfully Affect Our Lives

Imagine what it would be like to be intelligent, volitional beings without emotions. We'd be like computers, machines with no sensitivity, no ability to relate, no sorrows, and no joys. That doesn't sound very appealing to me! Our emotions were given not to *control* us but to *enable* us to enjoy life.

We often think we can solve our spiritual needs with a change in our physical circumstances. We take a little vacation. We go to the mall and buy a whole new wardrobe. For some, escape involves dependence on alcohol or other drugs—uppers and downers. For others, it's living for pleasure. But those remedies are just Band-Aids or temporary anesthetics. We are simply treating symptoms—and often making our circumstances even worse in the process. The truth is:

*God wants to heal our emotions by working through our spirits rather than by adjusting our circumstances.*

Escape never touches the root cause, which lies much deeper. God wants to heal the cause, not just relieve the symptoms of our emotional pain. And most importantly:

*God wants our emotional stability to be based on our relationship with Him rather than on physical or chemical stimuli.*

In the pages that follow, we'll study what the Bible says about God as our great Healer. We'll learn from biblical characters who experienced difficult emotions—selfishness, guilt, fear, worry, inability to forgive, anger, envy, rejection, greed, pride, feelings of inferiority, disappointment, discontentment, grief, and loneliness. We'll find the solution God offers to help us deal with these emotions effectively, and we'll study how to encourage each other. Finally, we will learn to do what we must do so that God can perform His miracles in the fragile network of our emotions as "He heals the brokenhearted and binds up their wounds" (Ps. 147:3).

# 2

## God, Our Healer

CAROLYN SHYLY CAME INTO MY OFFICE. With some diffi-culty, she explained that her sexual relationship with her new husband, Kevin, was, to say the least, uncomfortable. The young couple got along wonderfully in every other way. However, when the time came for physical intimacy, Carolyn invariably froze, wrestling with overwhelming emotional anguish.

Although she managed to submit to her husband's desires, the experience was always agonizing for her. She felt humiliated and ashamed during their time together, and she wasn't a good enough actress to fool Kevin. He was growing weary of her struggle and had encouraged her to seek help. When she was brutally honest with herself, she feared for her marriage.

As we talked, I studied Carolyn's quiet, pretty face. Although clearly concerned, she was surprisingly unemo-tional about the situation. I tried to understand her sexual inhibition, which clearly didn't emanate from a religious hang-up or some moral cause. Then, on a hunch, I asked, "Carolyn, is it possible that you were once sexually molested?"

At that point, her composure wilted. She looked stunned, and her eyes flooded with tears. "How did you know?" Carolyn whispered.

"Was it a family member?" I gently probed.

"No, no. It wasn't that. It was a friend of my parents, though. And when I told my mother, she called me a liar." At this point, Carolyn's voice broke.

"Did it happen more than once?" My heart sank, imagining how alone she must have felt.

"It went on for eight years, Vickie. It started when I was six years old. He finally moved away when I was fourteen, and that's when I told my mother. But she didn't believe me . . ."

Carolyn sobbed quietly for a few minutes. We continued our discussions on the subject for several weeks. At one point I said, "Carolyn, you were a victim. You were violated and exploited, and you were too young to know what to do. You can't blame yourself for what happened. Your parents' friend was the wrongdoer, and you need to place all the guilt where it belongs—on him. Not on yourself."

Finally I looked Carolyn in the eyes, and said to her, "That man has controlled your life since you were six years old. Are you going to let him control your future, too?"

Somehow, this got through to Carolyn. She was able to assign the full burden of guilt to him and to forgive him. Then we prayed together. "Lord," she said, "please heal me. Heal my memories so this situation doesn't haunt me for the rest of my life. And please teach me how to have a good sexual relationship with Kevin. He's been so patient . . ."

I was relieved and grateful to hear a few weeks later that positive changes were taking place in that troubled marriage. God, the Healer, had touched Carolyn and Kevin's lives.

## The Desire and the Power to Heal

Even though we've sought spiritual maturity through God's Word, prayer, fellowship, and obedience, some of us have been hindered by something that's kept us from enjoying emotional health and spiritual maturity. Like Carolyn, we've carried baggage from our past into our new lives. Destructive emotions have retarded or blocked our progress somewhere along the road to spiritual development.

Many of us have spent thousands of dollars for remedies that have not cured the source of our pain. Having tried so hard and struggled so mightily, it's wonderful to learn there is Someone who not only has the desire but also has the power to heal us. The Bible has much to say about God as our Healer.

God first revealed Himself as the Healer of His people in a strange little Old Testament incident described in Exodus 15. After four hundred years of bondage, the Israelites had just been delivered from Egypt by the mighty hand of God. They had seen plagues devastate the greatest civilization on the face of the earth. They'd had the exhilarating experience of passing through the Red Sea on a dry path while the waters stood firm as walls on either side. They had watched Pharaoh's elite corps of horsemen and chariots drown—the enemies who had terrorized them all their lives had been defeated. In this dramatic way God gave us a picture of the first step we experience today as He begins our emotional healing: freedom from the bondage of our past.

## God Offers Healing from the Past

When the Israelites saw that their bondage in Egypt was over and their former masters were powerless to enslave them again, they no longer had any reason to fear their former masters or obey them.

Much like those Israelites, when we put our faith in Jesus Christ we are freed from bondage to our old master, Satan. This liberation should also deliver us from the influence of the past on our emotions as well. But while this can happen right away, for most of us, it is a more gradual process. The first part of Exodus 15 is a song of praise to the Lord for His great victory over the Israelites' enemies. The people were on an emotional high. Then began their journey toward the Promised Land.

As the book of Exodus tells us, "Then Moses led Israel from the Red Sea and went into the Desert of Shur. For three days they traveled in the desert without finding water. When they came to Marah, they could not drink its water because it was bitter. (That is why the place is called Marah.) So the people grumbled against Moses, saying 'What are we to drink?'" (Exod. 15:22–24).

Three days in the desert without water, then the disappointment of undrinkable water, and God's people soon forgot His power and care for them. They could have said, "Look what God has already done for us! After all that, He'll surely find a way to provide water for us. We'll keep on trusting Him." But they didn't.

Instead the Israelites grumbled, a habit that persisted all through their journey. The text says they grumbled against Moses, but in reality, they were grumbling against the God who was leading them in the pillar of cloud and fire that moved before them. They were babies in their walk with their

God. Fortunately, He understood that and was very patient with them. Despite their complaining attitude He responded to their spokesman's plea: "Moses cried out to the LORD, and the LORD showed him a piece of wood. He threw it into the water, and the water became sweet" (Exod. 15:25).

Such a simple solution. So easy for God to do. And then: "The LORD made a decree and a law for them, and there he tested them. He said, 'If you listen carefully to the voice of the LORD your God and do what is right in his eyes, if you pay attention to his commands and keep all his decrees, I will not bring on you any of the diseases I brought on the Egyptians, for I am the LORD, who heals you'" (Exod. 15:26–27).

In the original language, God said, "I am Yahweh-Rapha, the Lord who heals you." *Rapha* means "to mend, to cure, to repair, to make whole."

God gave this promise to the ancient nation of Israel, but it includes a principle that still applies to us today:

***Emotional and spiritual health are by-products of obedience.***

Health is related to obedience both spiritually, physically, and emotionally. If we obey the commands against sexual immorality, we will not be infected by the sexually transmitted diseases that are rampant in our modern world. Meanwhile, our self-worth will not suffer from being used, cast off, and rejected.

If we obey the command to not covet, we will have a healthy attitude toward both relationships and possessions. We will be grateful for all that God has given us, whether much or little, and be immune to discontent, which works like acid in our emotions.

If we obey the commands against stealing, we will have healthy self-respect, a good name, and no criminal record.

If we honor our parents instead of rebelling against them, we will protect our family relationships.

There are innumerable healthy benefits to having a clear conscience. And God challenged His people to test Him and experience Him in a tangible way—He specifically said He would bless them with health if they obeyed His commands. But there's more to the incident at Marah for us to learn . . .

## The Power of the Cross

The instrument God used to heal the bitter waters was a piece of wood. Why not salt, the substance Elisha used hundreds of years later? Why not just a spoken word? Instead God directed Moses to throw a piece of wood into the water because *that* piece of wood pointed to another—the cross of Jesus Christ. The cross is the only way the bitter waters of our lives can be healed. In other words:

*The cross is God's remedy for emotional pain.*

## God's Additional Instruments of Healing

Hundreds of years before Christ's birth, the prophet Isaiah, who was prophesying about the work of the Messiah, said, "Surely he took up our infirmities and carried our sorrows, yet we considered him stricken by God, smitten by him, and afflicted. But he was pierced for our transgressions, he was crushed for our iniquities; the punishment that brought us peace was upon him, and by his wounds we are healed" (Isa. 53:4–6).

Isaiah said that Jesus would be taken up, carried, pierced, crushed, and wounded for our infirmities, our sorrows (emotions), our transgressions, our iniquities, our punishment.

Why did He do it? To bring us peace and healing: As

Isaiah said, *"By His wounds we are healed."* Some people teach that this means *physical* healing is guaranteed by Christ's atonement. But Peter interpreted this passage differently. He wrote, "He himself bore our sins in his body on the tree, so that we might die to sins and live for righteousness; by his wounds you have been healed. For you were like sheep going astray, but now you have returned to the Shepherd and Overseer of your souls" (1 Pet. 2:24–25).

Peter applies Isaiah's words to our *salvation*. God knew that we have to be healed spiritually for there to be emotional healing. The cross of Jesus Christ, where He bore our sins and took our punishment, made it possible for us to be reconciled to our God. It enabled us to come back to Him, cleansed and forgiven. His sacrifice for us brings us peace. That's spiritual and emotional healing, isn't it?

Maybe you're thinking, What about physical healing?

Remember that all healing is from God, whether it's through rest, sunshine, a healthy diet, the God-given skill of physicians or surgeons, or the miracles of prayer.

And as far as our emotions are concerned, God uses, in addition to the cross of Jesus Christ, at least four "instruments" to heal us: His Word, the power that comes from praising Him, the encouragement of His people, and the gift of a godly self-image. Let's look at each of these components of spiritual healing.

## God's Word Brings Healing to the Present

The healing power of God's Word is shown in, among other passages, Psalm 107, a song of praise to the Lord for His unfailing love for His people. He demonstrated this love by His deliverance when they called upon Him in their need: "Some became fools through their rebellious ways and suffered affliction because of their iniquities. They loathed all food and drew near the gates of death. Then they cried to the LORD in their trouble, and he saved them from their distress. He sent forth his Word and healed them" (Ps. 107:17–20).

Here we have people who were suffering affliction and physical, emotional, and spiritual sickness as a consequence of persistent rebellion against the Lord. Yet when they cried out to Him, He "sent forth His word and healed them."

How does God use His Word to heal?

Jesus demonstrated this godly gift beautifully when He was here on earth. He healed every possible affliction that humanity suffers, and He did so to demonstrate that He was the only One who could heal us from the root cause of all our troubles—sin.

Let's take a look at one specific incident. Luke 7 describes a Roman centurion whose servant had fallen ill and was near death. The centurion had heard about Jesus, and he had sent some elders of the Jews to ask Him for help.

Jesus responded to the request for healing by making His way toward the centurion's home, but before He could get there, another message from the centurion was brought to Him: "Lord, don't trouble yourself, for I do not deserve to have you come under my roof. That is why I did not even consider myself worthy to come to you. But say the word, and my servant will be healed. For I myself am a man under authority, with soldiers under me. I tell this one 'Go,' and he goes; and that one 'Come,' and he comes. I say to my servant, 'Do this,' and he does it" (Luke 7:6–8).

Jesus listened to this statement in amazement and told the crowd that He had never seen that kind of faith among the Jews. When the messengers returned to the centurion's house, they found that the servant had been healed.

This Roman warrior understood authority, and he knew Jesus had the authority to heal from a distance. Jesus could send forth His Word and heal, and that's just what He did.

But does He do it today? And if He does, how? What relation does the Word have to healing our emotions? To answer these questions, we need to look at the ways God uses His Word to heal us: our praise of Him.

## The Healing Power of Praise

One of the instructions we've received from the Lord says, "Rejoice in the Lord always" (Phil. 4:4). This is God's Word. But how can it heal?

Suppose you are filled with anxiety, fear, discouragement, or grief. Your future is uncertain. You have no job. There is terminal illness in your family. Your children have turned away from the Lord and are estranged from you. You are in deep grief because of the loss of someone you love.

In the midst of your troubles, this word is sent from God to heal you: "Rejoice in the Lord always."

You see, God is the only unchanging constant in our lives. When all else is gone—health, family, friends, money, position—God remains. "Jesus Christ is the same, yesterday and today and forever" (Heb. 13:8). Isn't that something to rejoice about? Not only is God present with us, but His Word also tells us that He loves us and nothing can separate us from that great unconditional love.

Another word from the Lord says, "Be joyful always; pray continually; give thanks in all circumstances, for this is God's will for you in Christ Jesus" (1 Thess. 5:16–18).

How can we apply this in a practical way? How about praying something like this:

"Lord, I feel terrible. I'm fearful, worried, lonely,

rejected, grieving. [You put in your own words.] But Your Word assures me that nothing here on earth, whether past, present, or future, can break my relationship with You through Jesus Christ.

"Since I'm going to live forever, my time on earth is a very small dot on the pages of eternity. I can rejoice in You because You will never abandon me. You will never stop loving me. You hear my prayers when I cry to You just as You did for Your people long ago.

"You have given me Your Word, and I choose to obey it. I rejoice in You. I praise You. I thank You for who You are and for what You have done for me."

Pray this prayer consistently, and I can practically guarantee there will eventually be a change in your emotions. But God knows we need help, both divine and human. And He provides that help.

## God's Holy Spirit Lives in Us

When we trusted Jesus Christ, He forgave our sins and called us to a new life of obedience to Him. He didn't say, "Now that I've forgiven you, clean up your act. Do your best. Try harder. You'll be able to change yourself." How hopeless that would be!

The wonderful fact is that He knew we couldn't change or heal ourselves in our own strength. He gave us Someone to help us. He gave us His Holy Spirit to take up residence in our hearts. He is the One who gives us new birth, makes us a new creation, and places us into the body of Christ. He is the One who makes us able to understand and apply Scripture (see 1 Cor. 2:12–13).

Romans 8 teaches us that the Spirit sets us free from slavery to sin. He is our new Master. He leads us in God's ways. He gives us assurance that we are God's children and can come into His presence with freedom and intimacy. He helps our weaknesses. He interprets our prayers, and He intercedes for us. Our part is to yield to His control, have our minds and hearts set on what He desires. Our part is to keep in step with His leading and trust Him to give us the ability to live to please God. He is the One who will work in our innermost being to give us the character of Jesus Christ, which is God's ultimate purpose for saving us and adopting us into His family. The family of God, other believers, is God's provision of the human help and companionship we need.

## God's Family Helps Us Heal

While I want to mention Christian friendship here as an instrument of God's healing, we'll postpone until chapter 18 an in-depth discussion. For now, it's sufficient to say that friends and support groups are keys to emotional healing; they are effective because we humans were created to need each other.

The Bible tells us that God loves and accepts us, yet we need the tangible demonstration of love and acceptance from people we can see, hear, and touch. If one part of the Christian body suffers, every other part suffers with it. So if you are in difficulty, don't be a loner. Reach out to Christian friends, support groups, or counselors, and allow them to help you. Give them the privilege and opportunity to pray for you.

## A Godly Self-Image Encourages Emotional Health

God also uses another powerful tool to keep us emotionally healthy. When we accept Jesus Christ into our lives, God gives us a new self-image in Christ. This healthy view of ourselves is only possible when we stop believing what our emotions tell us and start believing what God says about us.

For example, our emotions may tell us: "I don't think anyone has ever really loved me, so something in me must be unlovable. I feel like a loser. I don't feel that I'm a good Christian. I don't feel God's love."

In contrast, if we have a relationship with God because we have trusted Jesus Christ, this is what He wants us to hear: "I love you. You are now My child. I know all about you—past, present, and future—and I accept you. You are united with Christ. You are indwelt by the Holy Spirit. I will never abandon you, either in time or eternity."

Faced with those opposing kinds of self-talk, who are you going to believe, your feelings or God's Word? Not only must we believe God's evaluation of us, but we need to reject what our own faulty experiences and emotions tell us. As we consistently reject the negative impressions that we have believed for years and accept our new status as those whom God loves as He loves His own Son, our self-images will change.

Self-image *doesn't* change because we focus on pleasing ourselves, saying, "I'm doing something good for myself," and following all the other suggestions that feed self-centeredness. It changes because we choose with our wills to believe God and accept His love for us.

Yes, God can heal our emotions. He is our Healer. He wants to heal us. He wants to free us from the crushing emotional obstacles that hinder our growth to maturity. The wonderful fact is that He has the power to heal, and He has provided everything necessary for our healing:

- The cross of Christ,
- His Word,
- Rejoicing and praise,
- The Holy Spirit,
- His body, the church, and
- A new self-image in Christ.

# 3

## Serving the Self

MARLA SQUEEZED OUT A TEAR or two as the judge read the final divorce decree. She had initiated the separation and was looking forward to being single again. Of course it was sad, and she had a few lingering doubts about her decision. But soon Marla would have the opportunity to fulfill her destiny, just the way she had envisioned it a thousand times before. She would travel. She would paint. She would go to the theater and to gourmet cooking classes. She would have her own little condo, with a view of the city lights.

Her twenty-five-year marriage to Gary had been so confining—everyone knew he was a major control freak. All her friends agreed she was better off without him. Sure, he'd been generous with her, and he had made sure she had the best of everything. But Gary had never allowed her to "be herself." Instead, he was always telling her what to wear, what to cook, even what to think.

Now that the kids were away at college, it was her time to become the "real" Marla. Her son and daughter weren't at all happy about the divorce, but she shrugged off their protests. "You'll get over it," she had told them. "You have your lives, and now I have mine too."

The marriage settlement, as state law required, would give Marla half of everything, and in Gary and Marla's more-than-comfortable financial state, she would be set for life. Her intention was to dabble in real estate and to get much better acquainted with a certain man who'd caught her attention at her fitness center. He was young, great looking, and a free spirit, just like Marla. Her pulse speeded up at the thought of him.

"It's *my* turn to enjoy life," Marla whispered to no one in particular as she pulled her Mercedes out of the county court-house parking lot. "It's about time I did something for *me!*"

The popular psychology that had inspired and permitted Marla's divorce offers many familiar opportunities: Find yourself. Treat yourself with respect. Get to know the "real you." Take care of number one—if you don't, no one else will.

Have you noticed how much pressure we feel to think of ourselves *before* we think of others? It's our natural bent to do this, but we are now being brainwashed into believing that this is the only way to find fulfillment. Our culture is obsessed with the self. We are continuously encouraged toward self-fulfillment, self-gratification, and self-absorption.

This kind of philosophy doesn't mix well with true Christianity. In fact, it stands in stark contrast to the teaching of Jesus, who continuously taught self-sacrifice. He stated that we only find our souls when we lose them. And ultimately, He set an example for the ages by liter-ally laying down His life for others. With all that in mind, it seems logical to consider selfishness as a primary impediment to spiritual maturity. Since it often lies at the heart of our other emotional difficulties, let's take a serious look at selfishness before we move on to other obstacles that may be blocking our way to emotional and spiritual health.

## The True Needs of the Self

Abraham Maslow said, "Fulfillment and growth come from close attention to the *needs of the self.*" He taught that the self is a hierarchy of inner needs and that culture and tradition push people toward unauthentic selves. In other words, living for others is a trap. At the pinnacle of Maslow's hierarchy stood the self-actualized person who was virtually independent of culture or of troublesome ties to others.

The problem with this philosophy is that it's so easy to do. You don't have to teach children to be selfish or self-centered. One of our biggest challenges as parents is to train our sons and daughters to share, to be helpful, to be considerate, to think of themselves as part of a family where each person has responsibilities as well as privileges.

Satan had a basic strategy when he tempted our first parents in Eden. He intended to create skepticism about God in them, to turn their attention to themselves, and to stimulate their desire to please themselves rather than their Creator. This first manifestation of selfishness is still evident. In fact, it is thriving in today's world.

Selfishness greatly impedes our spiritual growth because the whole emphasis of Scripture is on our relationships to *others*. We are instructed to . . .

- Love others
- Serve others
- Honor others
- Help others
- Share with others
- Encourage others
- Admonish others
- Restore others

With that in mind, it's quite evident that if we persist in nurturing the immature selfishness we were born with, we will not grow into mature and fruitful believers.

## Abraham—God's Chosen Man

The story of Abraham (who was originally called Abram) and Lot draws a clear distinction between selfishness and the generosity that results from faith. God called Abraham to a great adventure in faith when He told him to leave family, friends, and homeland to go on a journey with God. He didn't know what his destination would be, but he believed God's promises, and he started out with everything he owned, bringing along his nephew Lot. And God gave him an amazing promise: "I will make you into a great nation and I will bless you; I will make your name great, and you will be a blessing. I will bless those who bless you, and whoever curses you I will curse; and all peoples on earth will be blessed through you" (Gen. 12:2–3).

When Abraham arrived in Canaan, the Lord told him, "To your offspring I will give this land" (Gen. 12:7). But the land was occupied by the Canaanites, and Abraham was a nomad traveling with his household and all of his livestock. He traveled from north to south exploring his family's future inheritance. Abraham "had become very wealthy in livestock and in silver and gold," (Gen. 13:2) and "Lot, who was moving about with Abram, also had flocks and herds and tents. But the land could not support them while they stayed together, for their possessions were so great that they were not able to stay together. And quarreling arose between Abram's herdsmen and the herdsmen of Lot" (Gen. 13:5–7a).

As both Abraham's and Lot's herds of livestock increased, the need for pasture and water did too. So their herdsmen started a range war. Abraham took the initiative to end it.

So Abraham said to Lot, "Let's not have any quarreling between you and me, or between your herdsmen and mine, for we are brothers. Is not the whole land before you? Let's part company. If you go to the left, I'll go to the right; if you go to the right, I'll go to the left" (Gen. 13:8–9).

I think I might have said, "Look, Lot, God told *me* to come here; He said He would give *me* this land. I've just let you come along out of the goodness of my heart. But if you can't keep your hired help from attacking mine, you'd better go back to Haran or Ur. This land is *mine*. God said so."

Instead, recognizing that they needed to separate, Abraham graciously gave Lot first choice of the land that lay before them. As he did so he demonstrated a powerful principle:

*We can be generous when we believe God's promises.*

There may be temporary detours on our paths, but when we entrust our lives to God, we needn't demand everything we think we have coming to us.

When I see how Lot responded to Abraham's generous offer, I'm reminded that sometimes those detours can contain some pretty sharp curves. Considering his uncle's generosity, "Lot looked up and saw that the whole plain of the Jordan was well watered, like the garden of the LORD. . . . So Lot chose for himself the whole plain of the Jordan and set out toward the east. The two men parted company" (Gen. 13:10–11).

Clearly, Lot should have said, "No, Uncle Abraham, you choose first. God promised this land to you. I appreciate your bringing me with you. There's room for both of us, so I'll take my family and flocks in the opposite direction from where you choose." However, Lot thought only of what was best for himself. We learn from Lot that selfishness is focused on the temporal and the material.

Lot saw that the plain was watered by the river and was lush and green. From the looks of it, he'd never have to worry about water or pasture for his flocks. So he chose for himself the whole fertile plain of the Jordan. He thought only of the material and temporal advantages of living there. But we get a foreshadowing of the consequences of his selfish choice in the next verses, which tell us that Abraham "lived in the land of Canaan, while Lot lived among the cities of the plain and pitched his tents near Sodom. Now the men of Sodom were wicked and were sinning greatly against the LORD" (Gen. 13:12–13).

## Selfishness Does Not Consider Spiritual Hazards

Lot pitched his tents near Sodom, unconcerned that Sodom was notorious for its evil—a city whose inhabitants were wholly given over to homosexual perversion. Lot didn't calculate their influence on his family or on himself. He just wanted that nice, green valley for his flocks. The selfish person only thinks of the here and now.

Meanwhile, Lot's choice didn't change God's plans for Abraham one little bit. He simply continued to reaffirm His promise to Him. After Lot left, God told Abraham, "Lift up your eyes from where you are and look north and south, east and west. All the land that you see I will give to you and your offspring forever. I will make your offspring like the dust of the earth, so that if anyone could count the dust, then your offspring could be counted. Go, walk through the length and breadth of the land, for I am giving it to you" (Gen. 13:14–17).

As we reflect upon the story of Abraham and Lot's dramatically contrasting attitudes and behaviors, we learn some priceless principles about selfishness and unselfishness.

Throughout the rest of the chapter, let's take a closer look at the way this ancient story reveals how these powerful principles still work to help us achieve emotional growth.

## Unselfishness Causes Us to Be Discriminating about the Source of Our Wealth and Advantage

Lot got into a great deal of trouble because of his selfish choices. Genesis 14 describes four kings who warred against five other kings in that area. Sodom was one of the defeated cities, and the victors carried loot and captives away with them. Guess who was included! "They also carried away . . . Lot and his possessions, since he was living in Sodom" (Gen. 14:12).

So Lot was now living *in* Sodom. Apparently he considered the material advantages more important than the moral and spiritual concerns for his family in that environment.

When Abraham received news of Lot's capture, he could have said, "It serves him right. Let him take the consequences!" But that wasn't Abraham's style. Instead, he mustered 318 trained men from his own household and pursued the victorious kings until he recovered all the goods and people they had captured, including Lot.

When Abraham returned, the king of Sodom rushed out to meet him. All of the loot and the people Abraham had rescued rightfully belonged to Abraham. But a king couldn't be a king without people. So he approached Abraham to cut a deal, suggesting, "Give me the people and keep the goods for yourself."

But Abraham answered him, "I have raised my hand to the LORD, God Most High, Creator of heaven and earth, and have taken an oath that I will accept nothing belonging to you, not even a thread or the thong of a sandal so that you will never be able to say, 'I made Abram rich'" (Gen. 14:21–23).

What an opportunity for Abraham to multiply his wealth! But he resisted the temptation. He was determined to let God alone be the source of his prosperity. That's what I meant when I said unselfishness causes us to be discriminating about the source of our wealth and advantage. Abraham would never let anyone, especially the depraved king of Sodom, have the right to say he was the one who made Abraham rich.

Abraham could be unselfish and generous because of his faith in God's promises of blessing. Abraham had his eyes fixed on eternity.

There are good ways and bad ways to accumulate wealth. As Christians, we must be willing to forego the fast buck that might be legal but is really unethical or ruthless. We are to avoid being users of people, and we're not to be opportunists who cash in on others' misfortunes. Instead, we trust God to give us what we need.

## Unselfishness Includes Intercession for Others

When we're unselfish, we put others' needs ahead of our own; this includes praying on their behalf. Again, this is demonstrated in the story of Abraham and Lot.

Many years after the Sodom incident, Abraham's unselfish concern for his selfish nephew was revealed again when Abraham interceded with God on Lot's behalf. Despite Lot's selfishness, Abraham had never stopped caring for him. He interceded for Lot when three visitors arrived at Abraham's camp. Although they looked like ordinary men, they were really the Lord and two angels.

As was his custom, Abraham treated the strangers with lavish hospitality. Soon Abraham realized who his guests were, and he heard from them that Sodom was to be destroyed. Realizing that impending disaster was about to fall on Lot, he pleaded for Lot's life. Abraham persisted in asking for God's mercy on his nephew until he was assured that Lot would not be destroyed. At that point, the visitors left Abraham, and two of them headed for Sodom.

## Selfish Ambition Causes Compromise

The next part of the story shows how Lot's selfishness gradually caused him to compromise his beliefs and his standards as he became enmeshed in the prevailing culture: "The two angels arrived at Sodom in the evening, and Lot was sitting in the gateway of the city. When he saw them, he got up to meet them and bowed down with his face to the ground. 'My lords,' he said, 'Please turn aside to your servant's house. You can wash your feet and spend the night and then go on your way early in the morning.'

"'No,' they answered, 'we will spend the night in the square.'

"But he insisted so strongly that they did go with him and entered his house. He prepared a meal for them, baking bread without yeast, and they ate. Before they had gone to bed, all the men from every part of the city of Sodom—both young and old—surrounded the house. They called to Lot, 'Where are the men who came to you tonight? Bring them out to us so that we can have sex with them'" (Gen. 19:1–5).

This passage tells us a lot, not only about the debauchery that permeated the city of Sodom, but also about how much Lot had acclimated to that city. He was now an important person in Sodom. We know this because the angels found him sitting at the city gate, where business and legal matters were conducted. The rulers of the city sat in the gate.

Have you noticed Lot's progression? First he pitched his tent near Sodom. Then he moved inside. Now he is a prominent member of Sodom's society. This couldn't have happened without some compromises on his part. He obviously knew what a wicked city he lived in, because he wouldn't let the two strangers camp out in the open.

## Selfish Ambition Brings Contamination

The next principle revealed in this story is how Lot's selfish ambition caused him to be contaminated by the sinfulness that surrounded him. This ugly chapter in the book of Genesis gives us an accurate picture of what still happens today when homosexuality is an accepted, alternative lifestyle. As Christians we must be compassionate toward these individuals, but let's never waver from the biblical posture that homosexuality is a sin that God despises and judges.

As the story continues, we see how Lot himself was polluted by the immorality of Sodom. "Lot went outside to meet them and shut the door behind him and said, 'No, my friends. Don't do this wicked thing. Look, I have two daughters who have never slept with a man. Let me bring them out to you, and you can do what you like with them. But don't do anything to these men, for they have come under the protection of my roof'" (Gen. 19:6–8).

So Lot offered his two daughters to the rapists. Protecting strangers was more important to him than protecting his daughters. It boggles the mind. Meanwhile, the Sodomites made no attempt to hide the contempt they had for Lot.

"'Get out of our way,' they replied. And they said, 'This fellow came here as an alien, and now he wants to play the judge! We'll treat you worse than them.' They kept bringing pressure on Lot and moved forward to break down the door.

"But the men inside reached out and pulled Lot back into the house and shut the door. Then they struck the men who were at the door of the house, young and old, with blindness so that they could not find the door" (Gen. 19:9–11).

The angels then urged Lot to get his family out of Sodom because God was going to destroy it. When he warned his daughters' fiancés of the impending judgment, they thought he was joking. He had no credibility with them, either.

Finally, the angels had to drag Lot, his wife, and his two daughters out of Sodom before the Lord destroyed it by raining down burning sulfur from heaven. The only reason Lot was rescued was because of his uncle Abraham's intercession; Genesis 19:29 says God "remembered Abram, and he brought Lot out of the catastrophe that overthrew the cities where Lot had lived." Lot's wife didn't fare so well; her ambivalence caused her to be turned into a pillar of salt.

## Selfish Choices Affect Our Descendants

Ultimately, Lot and his daughters got out of Sodom, but Sodom didn't get out of them. After the luxury of Sodom they were reduced to living in a cave. Then the story took another unbelievable twist. When Lot's daughters realized they had no prospects to marry and have children, they took turns getting their father drunk and having intercourse with him. Each of them bore a son as a result of that incest. The descendants of those sons, Moab and Ammon, were Israel's enemies all their days.

Our selfish sins influence our children, even when we think they don't notice. We are their primary role models, and our responsibility to model unselfishness and godliness is enormous. Lot made the selfish choice to prosper personally, but as a result of his choice he lost everything: his home, his possessions, his status, and his wife. And you might say he lost his daughters to the culture of Sodom. Can you imagine what it was like living with them after their sexual impropriety?

## Selfish Ambition Leads to Moral Failure

In the story of Lot and Abraham, we've seen how the selfish choices we make can lead us down the road toward not only material bankruptcy but also to moral and spiritual destruction. These are consequences we will face if we base our choices on material and temporal advantages. When we are focused only on the here and now, we will always choose what is best for ourselves. We often do so without a thought about the effect our actions may have on our future or on others, especially our families.

## We May Do Unselfish Things for Selfish Reasons

Sometimes, in our selfishness, we are blind to our own behavior, having convinced ourselves that we are being sacrificial. We can fool ourselves into thinking that we are unselfish because we are serving others. But it is entirely possible for us to play the servant's role with self-serving motives.

Even the disciples who lived with Jesus for over three years were infected with selfish ambition. They expected the Messiah to set up His earthly kingdom within their lifetimes, and they had great plans for themselves when He did. It's even more remarkable that at the exact time that Jesus predicted His death, James and John only thought of who would be top dog in the kingdom. These competitive young men even brought their mother into the act (see Matt. 20:17–28).

It's striking to contrast the self-seeking ambition of the disciples with the humility of their Lord. He left His throne in glory and came to serve, to give His life as a ransom for many. And He alone is to be our role model. We are not to model ourselves after people who achieve greatness through power, riches, or position. The greatest privilege we have on earth is not to rule over others but to serve them and give our lives to bring them to God.

## Selfish Ambition Comes from the World, the Flesh, and the Devil

Selfishness. Selfish ambition. The desire to be first. The longing to have the most. These are not the characteristics of a person under the control of God's Spirit. In fact, the opposite is true. Scripture tells us, "If you harbor bitter envy and selfish ambition in your hearts, do not boast about it or deny the truth. Such 'wisdom' does not come down from heaven but is earthly, unspiritual, of the devil. For where you have envy and selfish ambition, there you find disorder and every evil practice" (James 3:14–16).

Many sins have at their source selfishness and self-indulgence. As Paul warned the Galatians, "The acts of the sinful nature are obvious: sexual immorality, impurity and debauchery; idolatry and witchcraft; hatred, discord, jealousy, fits of rage, selfish ambition, dissensions, factions and envy; drunkenness, orgies, and the like. I warn you, as I did before, that those who live like this will not inherit the kingdom of God" (Gal. 5:19–21).

The person whose life is habitually characterized by these sins gives evidence that he or she is not a believer. But don't deceive yourself—believers aren't immune. The world, the flesh, and the devil exert all their energies and strategies to keep us from becoming the spiritually mature people God wants us to be.

## The Holy Spirit Delivers Us from Selfish Ambition

How can we overcome this attitude and emotion of selfishness that so easily controls us? It takes a commitment on our part, which we must live out day by day. Paul wrote, "So I say, live by the Spirit, and you will not gratify the desires of the sinful nature" (Gal. 5:16).

If we continue to follow the leading of the Holy Spirit, we will conquer our own selfish natures. This means we are to listen to His voice, obey God's Word, and follow godly impulses. Each time we do so, the temptation to be selfish is conquered, and it gets easier and easier to put this goal into practice. Then, without effort on our part, the Holy Spirit will produce fruit in our lives, providing evidence that He lives within us.

Notice how these godly characteristics affect our relationships with others and ourselves: "The fruit of the Spirit is love, joy, peace, patience, kindness, goodness, faithfulness, gentleness and self-control. Against such things there is no law. Those who belong to Christ Jesus have crucified the sinful nature with its passions and desires. Since we live by the Spirit, let us keep in step with the Spirit" (Gal. 5:22–25).

## Love for Others Cures Selfishness

Did you notice the first fruit mentioned? Love! *Agape* is the love God has showered upon us. And *agape* is the love He will implant in our hearts for others. It's more an action than an emotion. It does rather than feels. It's described perfectly in 1 Corinthians 13:5, which says, "Love is not self-seeking."

When you feel selfishness seeping into your actions and attitude, replace it with love. The way to stop the wrong behavior is to replace it with the right conduct. Paul tells us how to do this in Philippians 2:3–4: "Do nothing out of selfish ambition or vain conceit, but in humility consider others better than yourselves. Each of you should look not only to your own interests, but also to the interests of others."

## Our Selflessness Changes Others' Lives

Since we are all members of the body of Christ—children in God's family—the apostle Paul also exhorts us to be united in spirit, in purpose, and in love for each other.

Selfish ambition or vain conceit has no place in the life of the believer.

We will care about the people we work with and for. Maybe the boss is irritable and demanding because he or she is carrying a personal burden we know nothing about. Instead of resentment, we can make the boss's job less stressful by being the best, most considerate employee he or she has. And we'll certainly pray for the boss!

We will not always wait for our husbands to do something nice for us. Instead, we'll think of ways to make our homes safe havens for them. We'll welcome them with warmth, love, and laughter when they come home from a cold, demanding world, where they are often battered and bruised.

We'll give up some of our ambitions so we can be available to our children. It's a great sacrifice to put a career on hold to stay with babies, and the time seems to drag so slowly until they are teenagers—and eventually out on their own. But our sons and daughters need their mothers' presence, attention, and care. No one can substitute for Mother. The emotional and social consequences of not putting the interests of our children first will haunt us through future generations.

We'll also give of ourselves unselfishly by serving on boards and committees, not because of the power they give us, but because of a desire to do the best for the most people.

We'll speak up for what is right, even if it means personal loss.

We'll share with those in need.

We'll go a few blocks out of our way to bring someone to church who doesn't have a way to get there.

We'll work with a woman in a crisis pregnancy and help her through those long, lonely months.

We'll cook an extra casserole and bring it to the sick or grieving.

We'll tutor kids in the inner city and demonstrate the love of Christ to them, enabling them to acquire basic skills and encouraging their self-worth.

We'll let our adult children run their own lives, but we'll always be there to hear their joys and struggles, willing to help when they need us to.

We'll give a young mother some free time by taking the kids off her hands for a few hours.

We'll come alongside a woman or a couple having difficulties, and we'll work with them for months, even years, to save a life or a marriage.

We'll be happy to serve without applause because we are serving the Lord and want only His approval.

Perhaps as we've worked through this study on selfishness you have recognized that you've been living a very self-centered life. If so, confess your sin to the Lord and let Him cleanse you. Then be on the lookout for ways to serve other people. Ask the Lord to make you sensitive to their needs. Follow your good impulses and begin to experience the joy and fulfillment that comes from thinking of others rather than yourself.

The temptation to be self-centered is one we'll struggle with all our lives, but we can set our wills to follow the Lord's example. Like Him, we have been called to put the interests of others before our own. Let's begin today.

# 4

## The Burden of Guilt

AS AN EIGHT-YEAR-OLD CHILD, I had my first memorable experience with a guilty conscience. My father had died a few months before, and Mom, my sister, and I were still adjusting to his loss. Dad had always worn a gold pocket watch, and now that he was gone, that watch was a treasured family memento. Somehow the glass had come off, and my mother had carefully placed the watch on a countertop so she could have it repaired. She told both my sister and me not to touch it at all.

I was consumed with curiosity. When no one was around, I picked up the watch and opened it, examining it and experimenting with it. Suddenly, to my horror, I broke off one of the hands! With shaking fingers, I tried to put the watch back so it would look as if it hadn't been touched.

From that moment on, I kept out of my mother's way, but it wasn't long till she called me. I can still see her gazing into my eyes. "Did you touch Daddy's watch?"

"No!" I answered quickly.

Oh, the guilt! Now it was worse than ever. Not only had I broken the watch, but I had lied as well! It felt like a big rock in the middle of my chest. I stayed out of my mother's sight all day long, but my misery was intolerable. Eventually I decided I would rather take my punishment than live with those awful guilt feelings.

I went to Mom and confessed.

That spanking is the only one I remember from my childhood, and its severity had far more to do with my lies than with the damaged watch. But once it was over, my guilt was gone too. I had received the punishment I deserved. And my mother had forgiven me.

## A Guilty Human Pattern

Guilt is that awful feeling that hits us in the pit of the stomach when we know we have done wrong, and we'll do almost anything to get rid of it. Adam and Eve, our first parents, established a human pattern that continues to this day. First comes the cover-up. Then we play the blame game as we try to justify or rationalize our actions. We think that the more we can blame someone else, the less guilty we will feel.

Sometimes we try to escape from guilt through activities, alcohol, or drugs. Or we run to psychiatrists—but secular psychiatry has tried to solve the problem of guilt by saying there is no such thing as sin. Just ignore that guilty feeling, we're told, because it has no basis in reality. We try, but somehow we just can't pull it off. Why not?

We can't escape these feelings by ignoring them because God built into our natures a knowledge of right and wrong—a moral code. God's Word speaks of the moral conscience, which exists even within those who are not aware of His laws.

One example of this is described in Romans 2:14–15: "When Gentiles, who do not have the law, do by nature things required by the law, they are a law for themselves, even though they do not have the law, since they show that the requirements of the law are written on their hearts, their consciences also bearing witness, and their thoughts now accusing, now even defending them."

## God Gave Us a Conscience to Make Us Aware of Sin

There has never been a civilization on earth that didn't have laws—rules about right and wrong. Even though humankind hasn't always worshiped the living God, the moral codes of every civilization prove that there is an objective authority who has set a standard. The human conscience is evidence of God's existence and His standards for behavior.

God is the One we offend when we sin, and only He can provide a remedy for our sin and guilt. From the third chapter of Genesis on, He required animals to be sacrificed for human beings who wanted to have their sins forgiven. And the New Testament reminds us again, "Without the shedding of blood, there is no forgiveness" (Heb. 9:22).

But the blood of these thousands of animals could not *remove* sin. It only *covered* it, until the one perfect Sacrifice was made that completely satisfied the holiness and justice of God. When John the Baptist pointed to Jesus, he said in one sentence the purpose for His coming to earth: "Look, the Lamb of God, who takes away the sin of the world" (John 1:29).

## God's Only Remedy for Sin and Guilt Is Jesus

Jesus came to earth to die. He was the Substitute for us— He took our punishment in our place so we could be forgiven and made right with God. But what we don't always understand is that God also wants us to be free from guilt. We learn this from His Word.

## God's Forgiveness Includes a Cleansed Conscience

Through Christ, God has wiped our record clean. He wants us to know it, and to live in that freedom. We're told, "How much more, then, will the blood of Christ, who through the eternal Spirit offered himself unblemished to God, cleanse our consciences from acts that lead to death, so that we may serve the living God!" (Heb. 9:14).

When believers in biblical times put their faith in Christ, they acted like forgiven and cleansed people. Zaccheus, described in Luke 19, is a classic example. Everyone knew Zaccheus was a sinner—he worked for Israel's oppressor, the Roman government. In fact, Zaccheus was head of the equivalent to the Roman Internal Revenue Service. He levied the taxes Caesar required, and he was free to add whatever he wanted for himself.

When Jesus invited Himself to Zaccheus's house, He demonstrated publicly that He even accepted sinners as terrible as Zaccheus was perceived to be. Zaccheus responded by putting his faith in Christ as his Messiah. But notice how he gave evidence of it: "Zaccheus stood up and said to the Lord, 'Look, Lord! Here and now I give half of my possessions to the poor, and if I have cheated anybody out of anything, I will pay back four times the amount'" (Luke 19:8).

Zaccheus repented—he changed his way of life. He promised to make generous restitution to those he had cheated. The change was dramatic. That's why Jesus could say in response, "Today, salvation has come to this house." Zaccheus's new conduct was evidence of his new faith.

## Through Christ, Sin Is Gone Forever

The death and resurrection of Jesus Christ is God's eternal remedy for human sin. When we trust Him, He not only forgives our sins, but He also cleanses our conscience of guilt. What happens to our sins? Once God has forgiven them, they are:

- *Out of sight:* "You have put all my sins behind your back" (Isa. 38:17).

- *Out of mind:* "For I will forgive their wickedness and will remember their sins no more" (Jer. 31:34).

- *Out of reach:* "You will tread our sins underfoot and hurl all our iniquities into the depths of the sea" (Mic. 7:19).

- *Out of existence:* "I, even I, am he who blots out your transgressions, for my own sake, and remembers your sins no more" (Isa. 43:25).

Our sins are gone, removed from existence as if they had never happened in the first place. We can start our new life with a clean slate. And God gives us His Holy Spirit to empower us with new strength.

Have you been trying to make it on your own? Perhaps you have done things that have filled you with guilt, and you think if you're sorry enough and if you do enough good things, you can make up for the bad. No way!

## God Forgives Us by Grace through Faith in Christ

Scripture tells us we are washed clean and given new life through faith in Jesus Christ: "But when the kindness and love of God our Savior appeared, he saved us, not because of righteous things we had done, but because of His mercy. He saved us through the washing of rebirth and renewal by the Holy Spirit, whom he poured out on us generously through Jesus Christ our Savior" (Titus 3:4–6).

What wonderful words—kindness, love, and mercy! Have you trusted our kind and loving and merciful God alone to save you? If you haven't, talk to Him in your heart and tell Him you're through trying to *earn* your salvation. Trust in the Lord Jesus Christ alone for forgiveness, eternal life, and a cleansed conscience. There is no other way.

## Sin Damages Our Fellowship with God

So now we understand what happens to our sin when we ask God for forgiveness—it vanishes! But most of us have to ask another question: What happens when we sin *after* we have trusted Christ? Can a believer, a child of God, *lose* his or her salvation? Do we have to be saved all over again? If all our sins—past, present, and future—are forgiven because of Christ's death, why do we have to do anything at all?

The answer is this: When a believer sins, something happens that has to be dealt with. Our relationship with God cannot be broken, because we are His children by birth, but our fellowship with Him is damaged. Have you noticed that when you feel guilty because you've done something you know is wrong, you avoid praying or reading your Bible? You don't feel like coming to church, and you may not even enjoy being with your Christian friends as much as usual. These feelings are evidence that your fellowship with God is broken.

Because He loves us, God wants our fellowship with Him to be restored. And He has provided a way for us to continue being cleansed from guilt for sins we commit after our salvation. The apostle John tells us how it's done: "If we claim to be without sin, we deceive ourselves and the truth is not in us. If we confess our sins, he is faithful and just and will forgive us our sins and purify us from all unrighteousness" (1 John 1:8–9).

The trouble is, we often don't follow God's directions for our cure. Sometimes we wait a very long time before agreeing with God that we have sinned. All that time guilt eats its corrosive way into our conscience. David's story, in the Old Testament, is an excellent example of this process.

## The Story of David and Bathsheba

God spoke of David as a man after His own heart; He chose David to be king over Israel. From his teen years, David was devoted to God in an extraordinary way. He followed God's ways. He listened to godly counsel. And when he was a fugitive from King Saul for at least ten years, he constantly found his refuge in God, who rescued him again and again. David was a deeply spiritual man with a well-developed emotional capacity. He was also a man with normal human passions.

He was about fifty years old when he committed the sins that affected him for the rest of his life. Today this is called "going through midlife crisis." David saw another man's wife and lusted for her. It didn't matter that her husband was one of his trusted soldiers who was out on the battlefield fighting for him. David sent for Bathsheba and slept with her. Then, when she let David know she was pregnant, he ordered her husband Uriah to come home so he could sleep with her and thus make it look like the child was his. That didn't work, so David instructed his commanding general to put Uriah on the front of the battle lines so he would be killed.

Uriah died in battle, and after Bathsheba had finished her mourning period, David married her. The cover-up was in place. But then we read these ominous words at the end of 2 Samuel 11: "But the thing David had done displeased the LORD."

God knew all about David's behavior, and He would not let His beloved servant get away with such a flagrant and heartless abuse of power. During the unfolding of the story, about a year went by from start to finish—a year during which David seemed to be without a conscience at all. Remember, David was a believer, a man after God's own heart, a man to whom God had promised a lasting dynasty. His would be the royal line from which the Messiah would come. Didn't he feel guilty for sins as wicked as adultery and murder? Yes, but he had stifled his conscience. He wouldn't listen to the voice of the Holy Spirit. But he paid the price for his actions. Here's how he described his experience: "When I kept silent, my bones wasted away through my groaning all day long. For day and night your hand was heavy upon me; my strength was sapped as in the heat of summer" (Ps. 32:3–4).

So God sent the prophet Nathan to waken David's conscience with a story that appealed to his emotions. Nathan told him about a poor man who had only one little pet lamb, which he loved like a child. A rich man, who had many flocks of his own, stole this little lamb and made it into shish-kebabs for a dinner guest. Here's how David reacted to Nathan's story:

"David burned with anger against the man and said to Nathan, 'As surely as the LORD lives, the man who did this deserves to die! He must pay for that lamb four times over, because he did such a thing'" (2 Sam. 12:5–6).

Nathan looked into the face of his angry king who had just passed judgment on himself and said to David, "You are the man!"

How would David respond to the accusation and the punishment? He tells us his response in Psalm 32:5: "Then I acknowledged my sin to you and did not cover up my iniquity. I said, 'I will confess my transgressions to the LORD—and you forgave the guilt of my sin!'"

## Confession Is Required for Guilt to Be Removed

David made no excuses; he blamed no one else. He said, "I have sinned against the Lord."

You may be asking, What about his sin against Bathsheba and against Uriah? No, David saw his sin for what all sin is—an offense against the Lord. And he knew the punishment was just, because he knew the truth of this spiritual principle:

*Forgiveness does not cancel out the natural consequences of our sins.*

Nathan told David, "The LORD has taken away your sin. You are not going to die. But because by doing this you have made the enemies of the LORD show utter contempt, the son born to you will die" (2 Sam. 12:13).

The death of the child was just the beginning. David lived to see his son Amnon rape his half-sister, Tamar. Then David's son Absalom killed Amnon and later tried to seize David's throne, and he was also killed. In fact, from this time on, David's life deteriorated until the day he died. His one act of unbridled passion permanently marked his family and his kingdom. But his fellowship with God was restored. After Nathan came to him, David wrote Psalm 51, which eloquently describes his sin, his repentance, and his forgiveness.

## "I Can't Forgive Myself!"

When Elena's husband Sam made a major change in his profession, it put their marriage under a great deal of pressure. He got home late, left early, and barely spoke to Elena when they were together. Sam's stress level was astronomical, and he was irritable and rather mean to his wife. He was so wrapped up in his problems that, for the first time in their marriage, Elena wanted to make love when Sam didn't. She felt rejected and unattractive.

During this time, a married friend named Steve began to call Elena "just to talk." She openly welcomed Steve's calls. She was feeling lonely and abandoned, and she had come to the conclusion that Sam simply didn't love her anymore. It was a great relief to know she was still attractive to someone, and Steve was very open about his admiration for her.

Calls became lunches, and the lunches lasted into the afternoon. Before long, Steve and Elena were making love at least once a week. Fortunately, it didn't take more than a month for Elena's conscience to convict her of her adultery. Even though in some ways she felt entitled to her little fling, her Christian faith was too strong to allow her to carry on with Steve any longer. She broke off the affair and confessed it to her husband.

Sam forgave Elena and begged her to forgive him for his negligence and selfishness. They went to work in an attempt to heal their marriage. But Elena just couldn't get over the guilt she felt. When she came into my office, she kept repeating "I never dreamed I would ever do anything like that! I just can't forgive myself. I've hurt my husband so much, I don't know how he can forgive me. I cry all the time. I'm very depressed. I read the Bible and pray for hours, but I just can't get over it."

We talked for a long time. I reminded her of the promise expressed in 1 John 1:9. Of course she had confessed her sin over and over. But then I read Hebrews 9:14 to her: "How much more, then, will the blood of Christ, who through the eternal Spirit offered himself unblemished to God, *cleanse our consciences* from acts that lead to death, so that we may serve the living God!" (emphasis mine).

If God had forgiven Elena, yet she couldn't forgive herself, I suggested to her that she was setting herself up as a better judge than God. It's pride that tells us we would "never commit such a sin." We were each born with a sinful nature, and every one of us has the capacity to commit any sin in the book.

I instructed Elena to go back to 1 John 1:9 one last time and to agree with God that her actions were sin. Then I asked her to tell God she accepted His forgiveness and His cleansing of her guilt. "Elena," I explained, "we have to act with our *wills* to apply what God's Word says. Then He will eventually take care of our *emotions*."

Elena said she would do what I had suggested. She thanked me, and I didn't hear from her for about a month. Then she came to see me again.

She smiled, "I just want you to know that I'm doing much better. Oh, I have my moments, but I'm healing. You know, I listen to Christian radio for hours every day, and they talk about forgiveness, but I've never heard anyone mention Hebrews 9:14. That verse has changed my life!"

I've seen stories like Elena's happen many times. Some women carry a burden of guilt over a sin they committed years ago. They've confessed over and over, but they just don't think they deserve to be forgiven and have a cleansed conscience. *The missing link is the act of the will to accept what God offers: We accept God's forgiveness with an act of the will.*

## We Need a Clean Conscience to Serve God

Hebrews 9:14 provides an interesting insight about the result of our cleansing and forgiveness. God does this, the writer of Hebrews explains, "that we may serve the living God."

Guilt keeps us from serving God. Yet God can even use the sins we have committed to make us more effective in our work for Him. Only when we refuse God's provision for forgiveness, for cleansing, and for a new beginning are we incapacitated by our past sins. That's why it is important for us to remember:

### Satan wants us to be immobilized by guilt.

We have an enemy whose main purpose is to keep us from serving the Lord. In Scripture he is called the "accuser" of believers. If you continue to feel guilty for forgiven sins, you are hearing the voice of the enemy, not the Holy Spirit. Satan is a liar. Reject the fiery darts he shoots at your mind by holding up the shield of faith in the finished work of your Savior, and the devil will flee from you.

If guilt is the obstacle that has kept you from growing in your spiritual life, won't you lay down your burden at the cross? Accept God's forgiveness. Let Him cleanse your conscience. And commit yourself to living in obedience to God's Word and to the guidance of the Holy Spirit, who lives within you. Your burden of guilt will be lifted—once and for all.

# 5

~⊙⊙~

# Nothing to Fear
# But Fear

THERESA HAD A WONDERFUL JOB. She worked behind the scenes in a television studio and spent her days hobnobbing with celebrities, producers, and writers. Theresa was an extrovert and an exceptionally pretty redhead. She absolutely relished the thought of going to work every day—except for two problems. For one thing, she wasn't making as much money as she deserved. For another, and far worse, her boss was always trying to get her into bed with him.

Before she became a Christian believer, Theresa and her boss had been involved in an affair. He was handsome, witty, sophisticated—and married. Once she trusted Christ, Theresa made up her mind that she wanted to live a pure life. The only problem was that her boss wouldn't leave her alone. Hardly a day passed without some innuendo, some inappropriate gesture, some flirtatious come-on.

Since Scripture tells us to "flee from sexual immorality,"[1] I suggested that Theresa quit her job and find another. She was terrified! The thought of cutting off her income without anything lined up in advance seemed foolhardy to her, and she choked on the idea of "stepping out in faith." She was equally frightened by the prospect of ending up in some boring desk job, light-years away from the exciting world of television.

Theresa decided to tough out the situation with her boss. She simply avoided him as much as possible. But his persistent appeals made her feel compromised and impure. For a few more weeks, fear immobilized her. Every time she thought about walking into his office and saying, "I quit!" she felt sick to her stomach. Her heart pounded, and her palms got sweaty when she tried to imagine getting up one morning without a job.

But after many weeks of struggle, Theresa finally decided to quit. She called me, and with her voice shaking with apprehension, she confided, "I'll just do it. I'll trust God to give me another job. Please pray for me!"

Within two weeks of resigning, Theresa had a new job. Not only was it every bit as exciting as her original position, but it paid her nearly a thousand dollars more per month. By choosing to face her fear and overcome it, she ended up in a far better situation than the one she left.

## The Nature of Fear

Theresa's situation reminds me of a famous quote by an even more famous man. In 1933, the country was in a severe depression. The stock market had crashed four years before. People had lost their jobs and their homes. Savings were gone. There was no social security. People stood in bread lines for food. The threat of starvation and homelessness was constant. Fear pervaded the very atmosphere.

A new president was about to take office. After Franklin D. Roosevelt was sworn in, he gave his inaugural address. One of the things he said as he tried to bolster the morale of his disheartened countrymen has become immortal. He said, "We have nothing to fear but fear itself!"

What a profound statement! Roosevelt knew what fear can do. Fear paralyzes us. It causes ambition and courage to leak out and leaves us without resources to face even the simplest situations. Fear is defined as "an emotion aroused by threatening evil or impending pain, accompanied by a desire to avoid or escape it; apprehension or dread."

There are different kinds of fear. Some fear is caused by experiences from the past. For example, there are people whose self-confidence was so injured by an insensitive, unkind teacher that they fear drawing any kind of attention to themselves. This fear affects their relationships, their jobs, everything in their lives.

Others have been wounded by parents and their habitual violent responses.

And, of course, there are wives who cower in fear every time a drunken husband lurches through the door—a travesty on marriage.

Then there are the irrational fears—phobias, which no amount of reasoning seems to help. Fear of flying, fear of crowds, fear of heights, fear of germs, fear of hospitals. All of these fears can be serious obstacles to our growth into spiritual maturity. We won't be spiritually mature if we aren't emotionally mature. However, all fear is not bad. There is a kind of fear that is for our benefit.

## God Gave Us the Capacity for Fear

God built into us the emotional response of fear just as He did the ability to love.

Not long ago, my husband and I were on the tollway. I was driving when my husband suddenly shouted, "Watch out!"

A truck on my right was merging into our lane because the right lane was ending. He was almost on top of us. I immediately swerved to avoid him. Then I felt a tingling all through my body. Adrenaline had rushed in to help me respond to danger. Normal, healthy fear had served me well.

When we warn our children not to talk to strangers, not to go with strangers anywhere, not to let anyone touch their private parts, that comes from an honest fear that they may be molested or killed. When we lock our doors and install security systems in our homes, it is a wise reaction to the escalating crime in our communities.

These kinds of fears are realistic responses to the fact that we live in a fallen world. We can't control evil people or the ravages of nature. That kind of fear is a gift; God instilled it into us for our benefit.

## God Wants Fear to Protect, Not Imprison, Us

Fear is part of our Creator's loving provision for us. Properly controlled, fear protects us from harm and motivates us toward positive action. If you were to see a bear in the woods, you wouldn't go up and pet it—you'd flee as fast as you could. Your sensible fear protects you. Uncontrolled fear, however, can lock us into an emotional prison and stunt our personal and spiritual growth. Unrestrained fear darkens our lives; it colors everything we do. It is a great obstacle to our spiritual growth.

God's Word gives us His perspective about fear: "For God hath not given us the spirit of fear" (2 Tim. 1:7 KJV), and "Perfect love drives out fear" (1 John 4:18).

If God doesn't give us a spirit of fear and we know that He loves us perfectly, why are we still afraid? How can we be freed from the paralysis this kind of fear generates? We must learn to fight fear with fear—another kind of fear that is the antidote for our uncontrolled fears. It's called the *fear of the Lord.*

When we have the fear of the Lord, it means we look upon God with awe or reverence, an attitude accompanied by obedience, knowing, "The fear of the LORD is the beginning of wisdom" (Prov. 9:10).

## Fear of God Will Change Your Perspective

All our lives, we seem to alternate between the fear of people and circumstances, and the fear of the Lord. But the more we fear the Lord and trust His sovereignty, the less we will be at the mercy of our fears. It took the patriarch Jacob a lifetime to learn this lesson. I hope we can learn to adopt an attitude of fearlessness a little more quickly than he did!

Genesis 27 reveals the flawed relationships in Jacob's family—the family that God chose to be His instrument to bring salvation to the world. Take a few minutes to read the story. You'll see that Isaac, the father, was determined to give God's Abrahamic blessing to his favorite son, Esau.

Meanwhile, Isaac's wife Rebekah knew before her twins were born that God had chosen the younger son, Jacob, to receive the blessing. Rebekah instructed and conspired with Jacob, who was her favorite, to steal the blessing by disguise and lying. When Esau found out that his mother and brother had plotted against him and robbed him of his birthright, he "held a grudge against Jacob because of the blessing his father had given him. He said to himself, 'The days of mourning for my father are near; then I will kill my brother Jacob'" (Gen. 27:14).

***Jacob—A Man Who Lived in Fear.*** Following the deception, Jacob ran away from home because of a very real fear that Esau would kill him. From Esau's perspective, such a violent reaction would have been justified, and Jacob's guilty conscience confirmed it. But during Jacob's first night on the road, when he lay down on some stones to sleep, an amazing thing happened (see Gen. 28:10–15).

Scripture tells us Jacob had a dream in which he saw a ladder, or a stairway, leading from earth to heaven, with angels moving up and down it. Above the stairway stood the Lord. And the promises He made to Jacob were astonishing:

"I am the LORD, the God of your father Abraham and the God of Isaac. I will give you and your descendants the land on which you are lying. Your descendants will be like the dust of the earth, and you will spread out to the west and to the east, to the north and to the south. All peoples on earth will be blessed through you and your offspring. I am with you and will watch over you wherever you go, and I will bring you back to this land. I will not leave you until I have done what I have promised you."

God confirmed to Jacob that the covenant He had made with his grandfather Abraham would be fulfilled through Jacob's descendants. Jacob hadn't needed to lie and deceive to get the blessing. God had always intended to give it to him. In order for this promise to come true, he couldn't be killed by Esau. God also promised that He would be with Jacob wherever he went, and He would bring Jacob back to his homeland.

When he awoke from his dream, Jacob realized that God's presence had been there. He said, "How awesome is this place! This is none other than the house of God; this is the gate of heaven" (Gen. 28:17).

Jacob responded with reverence and a genuine fear of God. The next morning he built an altar and made a vow: "If God will be with me and will watch over me on this journey I am taking and will give me food to eat and clothes to wear so that I return safely to my father's house, then the LORD will be my God and this stone that I have set up as a pillar will be God's house, and of all that you give me I will give you a tenth" (Gen. 28:20–22).

Notice the "if" and "then." This was a conditional vow. But hadn't God just made *unconditional* promises to Jacob? Yes, but Jacob had a long way to go before he would trust Him completely. This was the beginning of his personal walk with God. He was a baby in his faith.

This kind of "bargaining" is so familiar to us today. We tell the Lord, "If You get me out of this situation, I'll trust You." Or, "If You heal my child, I'll serve You." Or, "If You'll give me a good job, I'll give You 10 percent of my income." It's as if we are trying to bribe God to save us from the ups and downs of life.

## God's Promise of Unfailing Love

I remember my first and only experience on a roller coaster. I was about twenty years old when I rode the Cyclone at Coney Island. When we reached the top and started down that track at what seemed like two hundred miles an hour, I was terrified. I promised the Lord, "If You get me out of this alive, I will never get on a roller coaster again." Believe me, that's been an easy promise to keep!

Did God bring me safely through just because I made that promise, or was He going to do it anyway? Of course He would have protected me, promise or no promise. All the time we are setting up our conditions, God says, "I love you unconditionally. I will never leave you. I'm in control of the universe. Don't you know I want to take care of you? You don't have to bribe Me with promises."

After the revelation of God's presence along the way, Jacob reached his mother's family and fell into the clutches of his Uncle Laban. Laban was an even bigger liar and cheat than Jacob. After spending twenty years there, Jacob had married Laban's two daughters and had twelve children. Then God spoke to him again: "Go back to the land of your fathers and to your relatives, and I will be with you" (Gen. 31:3).

It was clearly God's time for him to go back home, but Jacob was afraid. This time, Jacob was afraid that Laban would try to hinder him from leaving. So he took his family, his flocks, and all his possessions and ran away. He didn't even say good-bye.

Do you see Jacob's problem? Fear of man overpowered his fear and reverence for God. God had promised to take him safely home, and he was obeying God by going back. But he couldn't trust God to handle the Laban situation! Therefore, instead of leaving behind a pleasant ending to their relationship, Laban and Jacob parted on a hostile, suspicious note, promising retaliation if either one harmed the other. Why does God let things like this happen to His people? The answer is another spiritual principle that we must learn to accept and live with, trusting that God knows what He's doing:

*God permits fearful circumstances even when we are doing His will.*

Many Christians have the misconception that if we are living to please God, nothing will touch our lives to make us feel afraid. They say, "Doesn't God want us to be happy?"

The answer to that question is "No!"

Personal happiness is *not* what God has promised; He gives us His joy, which has its source in our relationship with Him. He never guarantees that our circumstances and relationships will not cause us stress, pain, and fear. In fact, difficult situations are the very things that force us to rely on His presence and to substitute fear of God for our fear of man.

## Awareness of God's Presence Calms Fears

There's a direct connection between God's presence and the absence of fear. When we put the things we fear under His authority, those things lose their power to terrorize us. We have to remind ourselves that everything touching us is filtered through God's wisdom and love. We can trust Him for the strength and protection we need.

As for Jacob, he successfully got away from Laban, but another threat loomed in the distance. What about Esau? Did Esau still want to kill Jacob? How should he approach his estranged brother? God wanted Jacob's faith in Him to grow, so He did something very special for him. The book of Genesis continues the story:

"Jacob also went on his way, and the angels of God met him. When Jacob saw them, he said, 'This is the camp of God!'" (Gen. 32:1–2).

Angels were traveling with him, protecting him and his

family. Wasn't God good to let him actually see these super-natural beings sent to quiet his fears and encourage his faith? This time there was to be no running away.

Jacob sent word to his brother Esau that he was returning from his years with Laban, bringing with him cattle and donkeys, sheep and goats, and many servants. He said, "I am sending this message to my lord, that I may find favor in your eyes."

When the messengers returned from delivering Jacob's message they said, "We went to your brother Esau, and now he is coming to meet you, and four hundred men are with him" (Gen. 32:5–6).

*Four hundred men?* That amounted to a small army! Poor Jacob was terrified all over again. First, he made plans to protect at least half of his possessions. Jacob always had a Plan B; trusting God still came very hard for him. But he did remember to pray, and his prayer alternated between reminding God of His promises and expressing his own real fears (see Gen. 32:9–12). Jacob's prayer gives us a practical pattern to follow when we are afraid:

**Focus on God's promises, not on your fears.**

Most of us aren't all that different from Jacob, and when we focus on our circumstances, we are often overwhelmed with fear. Instead, we should remember God's promises and pray them back to Him. We can tell Him our fears, ask for His help, and tell Him that we trust Him.

Let's look at a real-life possibility. Suppose your mammogram has revealed a lump. You must have a biopsy. The possibility of cancer fills you with the fear of death. How can God's Word help you? Hebrews 2:14–15 gives us hope: "Since the children have flesh and blood, he too shared in their humanity so that by his death he might destroy him who holds the power of death—that is, the devil—and free those who all their lives were held in slavery by their fear of death."

Fear of death—and the process that leads to it—is slavery to Satan. And Jesus Christ has made Satan powerless over the ones He has redeemed. As King David said, "When I am afraid, I will trust in you" (Ps. 56:3). Notice David didn't say *if* I am afraid, but *when*. God knows we will be afraid. That's why He gives us a choice:

***Fear is an emotion. Trust is an act of the will.***

Fear cancels out trust, and vice versa. So your prayer might sound something like this: "Lord, I'm praying that this lump is benign. I'm afraid of dying from cancer. But Hebrews 2:14 tells me that Jesus died to free me from slavery to the fear of death. So whatever the results are, I'm going to trust You and enjoy the peace and freedom You have given me. I will not let fear of sickness and death erode my trust in You."

Like Jacob, we are able to choose with our will to believe God and not be afraid. As it is for us, it was very hard for Jacob to just trust the Lord and not make plans of his own just in case God didn't come through.

Part of Jacob's Plan B was bribing Esau with gifts, hoping to "pacify him." Hadn't he just asked God to save him? Yes. But Jacob was a born manipulator. He just had to keep his finger on all the buttons. Even though he had called on God for help, he still depended on his own schemes. That night he had a climactic struggle with God—an event that marked him for the rest of his life.

While Jacob was alone, Scripture says a "man" wrestled with him all night. When the man saw that he could not overpower Jacob, he "touched the socket of Jacob's hip" and crippled him. Then he said, "Let me go, for it is day-break."

But Jacob, apparently aware that he was wrestling with God Himself, replied, "I will not let you go unless you bless me."

Then the man asked Jacob his name, and when Jacob told him, the man said, "Your name will no longer be Jacob, but Israel, because you have struggled with God and with men and have overcome."

Then Jacob asked the man his name.

But the man replied, "Why do you ask my name?" And instead of telling Jacob his name, Genesis 32:29 says, "Then he blessed him there."

Jacob decided to call the place "Peniel, saying, 'It is because I saw God face to face, and yet my life was spared'" (Gen. 32:28–30).

Surely now, after this amazing encounter, Jacob's dependence on himself and his own devices would end. But old habits are hard to break. Instead of simply trusting in the Lord who had blessed him, Jacob divided his family in order of preference—just in case. Then he humbly approached the brother he had wronged and feared so terribly. And what did Esau do? "Esau ran to meet Jacob and embraced him; he threw his arms around his neck and kissed him. And they wept" (Gen. 33:4).

A warm embrace and a kiss instead of a sword! It seems that God had also worked on Esau's heart during their twenty-year separation. Jacob had never needed to be afraid throughout that long journey. It hadn't been necessary for him to devise all those schemes to appease Esau. Esau was no longer his enemy. But although Esau invited Jacob to come to his home and even offered to escort him there, Jacob still couldn't trust him. He again resorted to subterfuge and continued his journey home without visiting Esau.

## A Last Word of Promise

God's final assurance to Jacob comes almost forty years later, in Genesis 46. The domestic tragedy of jealousy, betrayal, and deceit that involved Jacob's son Joseph and his brothers had kept Jacob grieving for twenty-two years. Now Joseph was reunited with his brothers, and he ordered them to bring their father, Jacob (renamed Israel after he wrestled with God), and all their families to Egypt so he could feed them during the remaining five years of famine. His old father was overjoyed to know that Joseph was alive. "So Israel set out with all that was his, and when he reached Beersheba, he offered sacrifices to the God of his father Isaac.

"And God spoke to Israel in a vision at night and said, 'Jacob! Jacob!'

"'Here I am,' he replied.

"'I am God, the God of your father,' he said. 'Do not be afraid to go down to Egypt, for I will make you into a great nation there. I will go down to Egypt with you, and I will surely bring you back again. And Joseph's own hand will close your eyes'" (Gen. 46:1–3).

God knew his fearful old friend Jacob so well, and He loved him so much. His first words to him were, "Don't be afraid." This time, Jacob had no Plan B. He didn't worry that Pharaoh might kill him. He just trusted the Lord. Seventeen years later, as he blessed his sons on his deathbed, Jacob gave this testimony: "May the God . . . who has been my shepherd all my life to this day, the Angel who has delivered me from all harm—may he bless these boys."

## God Monitors Fearful Circumstances

When my daughter Helene was in labor, she was hooked up to monitors that gave a continual record of her heart rate, her blood pressure, and her contractions. There was also a monitor on the baby, recording her heart rate as well. The minute anything looked a little irregular, a doctor was there, prescribing what was needed to correct it.

In much the same way, God monitors our circumstances and our reactions to them. He hears every little beep and sees every point of stress on our faith.

The words, "Fear not" appear one hundred times in the Bible. This doesn't mean there are no real and present dangers in our lives—things that are sensible to fear. What it does mean is that God does not want us to be immobilized by fear. Instead, He wants us to trust His presence, His love, His protection, and His sovereignty over our fearful circumstances. He wants us to focus on His promises rather than on the circumstances that terrify us. He knows just what we can bear. He also knows how much each difficult situation will stretch us and deepen our faith in Him.

### God Delivers Us from our Fears

"I sought the LORD, and he answered me, he delivered me from all my fears. . . . The angel of the LORD encamps around those who fear him, and he delivers them. . . . Fear the LORD, you his saints, for those who fear him lack nothing" (Ps. 34:4, 7, 9).

# Nothing to Fear But Fear

What fears have kept you imprisoned? Don't allow uncontrolled fear to keep you from growing to maturity in your relationship with God. Christ died to set you free from the worst fear—fear of death. And He lives to deliver you, to comfort you, to help you through all the fearful circumstances of life. You have a choice to trust God and not be afraid or to be afraid and not trust God. Which will it be?

*Thou art my Lord Who slept upon a pillow.*
*Thou art my Lord Who calmed the furious sea.*
*What matter beating wind and tossing billow*
*If only we are in the boat with Thee?*

*Hold us in quiet through the age-long minute*
*While Thou art silent and the wind is shrill.*
*What boat can sink when Thou, dear Lord, art in it?*
*What heart can faint that resteth on thy will?*

*Amy Carmichael*[2]

# 6

## Weary of Worry

FOR AS LONG AS I CAN REMEMBER, I have disliked motorcycles. So, as you can well imagine, I was not at all pleased to learn that my adult son Robert had purchased a motorcycle as his only means of transportation. Visions of ghastly accidents haunted me. Robert lived two hundred miles away, and I was quite certain that if he had a terrible crash, our phone number would not be with his identification. So, not only would he be brutally wounded, but it would be days—even weeks—before we found out about it.

My anxiety was unending. Every time I saw a motorcycle on the road, I'd think of Robert. Fear and anxiety chilled me; a sick feeling crept into my body. Of course I knew I could not continue to survive in such a state of constant agitation. Somehow, I had to choose to apply my Christian faith to this source of continuous worry.

My way of doing this was through prayer. I decided that when I saw a motorcycle and worry tried to grip me, I would simply pray. I rejected mental images of twisted metal and broken limbs and instead prayed for Robert's safety and health, as well as for the person on the motorcycle I was seeing. Before long, my worry was replaced with the peace that comes only with prayer. It became quite a habit. In fact, to this day, whenever I see a motorcycle, I still automatically pray for my son.

## Strangled by Worry

Are you a worrier? What do you worry about? Do you worry that you won't be able to pay your bills? Do you worry about your children when they're out of your sight? Do you feel anxiety about your marriage? Do you worry about your health? Are you anxious about the future because you're facing a new job, a move to another city, having a new addition to your family? Maybe you just worry because it is a habit.

What *is* worry?

Worry is to be uneasy in the mind, to feel anxiety about something, to fret. Interestingly, it comes from an Old English word that means "to strangle."

What an appropriate derivation! Worry strangles our peace of mind and our enjoyment of life. There's a direct connection between fear and worry. Sometimes they may be interchangeable. Worry affects us mentally, emotionally, spiritually, and physically. Dr. Charles Mayo said, "Worry affects the circulation, the heart, the glands, the whole nervous system, and profoundly affects the health."

God instructs us not to worry, and Scripture overwhelms us with reasons for not being anxious. Let's look at an interesting incident in the Old Testament that gives us a powerful defense against worry.

In 2 Kings 6, the king of Aram (now the nation of Syria) was at war with the northern kingdom, Israel. In the secrecy of his war room, he would plan to attack Israel and take her by surprise. But every time he arrived at the place he had chosen, he would find Israel's army was already there defending it. He was infuriated. The only reasonable answer was that he had a spy in his camp. When he confronted his officers with the charge they answered, "'None of us, my lord the king, . . . but Elisha, the prophet who is in Israel, tells the king of Israel the very words you speak in your bedroom.'

"'Go, find out where he is,'" the king ordered, 'so I can send men and capture him.' The report came back: 'He is in Dothan.' Then he sent horses and chariots and a strong force there. They went by night and surrounded the city.

"When the servant of the man of God got up and went out early the next morning, an army with horses and chariots had surrounded the city. 'Oh, my lord, what shall we do?' the servant asked" (2 Kings 6:12–15).

## An Army of Angels

Imagine waking up and finding your city surrounded by an enemy army! Elisha's servant was worried sick, terrified. But through this frightening experience, he learned a wonderful truth.

"'Don't be afraid,' the prophet answered. 'Those who are with us are more than those who are with them.'

"And Elisha prayed, 'O LORD, open his eyes so he may see.' Then the LORD opened the servant's eyes, and he looked and saw the hills full of horses and chariots of fire all around Elisha" (2 Kings 6:16–17).

Elisha didn't have a worry in the world! God had sent an angelic army to protect his servant. After surveying that breathtaking display of power, he knew what the outcome would be. He was able to show mercy to the enemy soldiers because God had rendered them harmless. From this, we learn a key principle:

*Introducing God into the equation changes the odds, no matter how frightening the situation looks.*

Maybe you're thinking, *Well, that's the Old Testament. There were all kinds of miracles then. That doesn't apply to this day and age.* That's not true. This incident is an illustration of a New Testament principle described in 2 Cor. 10:3–5: "For though we live in the world, we do not wage war as the world does. The weapons we fight with are not the weapons of the world. On the contrary, they have divine power to demolish strongholds. We demolish arguments and every pretension that sets itself up against the knowledge of God, and we take captive every thought to make it obedient to Christ."

Contrary to the saying, "What you see is what you get," what we see is *not* all there is. Intense warfare is constantly being waged in the spirit world. Like Elisha, we have angels protecting us too. This is one reason we should not worry. Hebrews 1:14 and Matthew 18:10 inform us that we have guardian angels—spirit beings whose job it is to serve us.

God has also given us the armor and the weapons necessary to defeat our powerful enemies. Ephesians 6:10–18 is a wonderful passage depicting our spiritual armor as the armor of a Roman soldier. Every piece of that armor is defensive except one. The only offensive weapon we have is "the sword of the Spirit, which is the word of God." God's Word combined with prayer defeats our unseen enemies.

Do you see why fear and worry are so unnecessary for the believer? God is on our side. He has given us what we need for peace of mind, protecting us from the cancer of worry. He knows everything that's going on, just as He knew what the Syrian king was plotting in his war room. He can prevent or permit whatever He wants, and sometimes He allows things that will hurt us. Why? Because if we trust Him, He will work them for our good. God is our Father, and we are His responsibility, just as we earthly parents are responsible for our children. Here's another important principle:

**Worry happens when we assume responsibility God never intended us to have.**

You may be thinking, *If we don't worry, how will I feed and clothe my family? Isn't worry a good motivator? Doesn't it help to keep us on track?* The answer to these questions is a resounding NO!

When Jesus was here on earth He addressed the issue of worry as it relates to all of our lives. First He dealt with our motives and goals, urging us, "Do not store up for yourselves treasures on earth, where moth and rust destroy, and where thieves break in and steal. But store up for yourselves treasures in heaven, where moth and rust do not destroy, and where thieves do not break in and steal. For where your treasure is, there your heart will be also" (Matt. 6:19–24).

## Make God the Master You Serve

If your focus is on making money and providing for your own future, then your eyes are focused on the wrong goal, and you are in spiritual darkness. Your love of money and your devotion to it will steal your heart; it will replace your love for God and devotion to Him. Jesus said love of money and love of God cannot coexist in the human heart. Having said this, Jesus went on to tell us that our heavenly Father knows our material needs and will provide them: "Therefore I tell you, do not worry about your life, what you will eat or drink; or about your body, what you will wear. Is not life more important than food, and the body more important than clothes? Look at the birds of the air; they do not sow or reap or store away in barns, and yet your heavenly Father feeds them. Are you not much more valuable than they?" (Matt. 6:25–27).

Don't worry about your life. God feeds the birds, and you are much more valuable than they are. So much for the spotted owl! This might come as news to some people today, but people and animals are not equally valuable. People are made in God's image. If God provides food for all His creatures, surely He will care for the basic needs of His own children.

"And why do you worry about clothes? See how the lilies of the field grow. They do not labor or spin. Yet I tell you that not even Solomon in all his splendor was dressed like one of these. If that is how God clothes the grass of the field, which is here today and tomorrow is thrown into the fire, will he not much more clothe you, O you of little faith?" (Matt. 6:28–30).

Jesus calls the worrier, "O you of little faith." We don't usually think of worry as a lack of faith, but that's how God sees it.

## Your Heavenly Father Knows What You Need

When your child was born, you didn't wait for it to tell you it needed milk or clothes or that it needed a diaper change. Of course not! You knew what your baby needed, and it was your joy to provide it. With far greater understanding, our heavenly Father knows what we need, and He is certainly a better parent to His children than we could ever be to ours.

Our Father's desire is that we simply seek to please Him. That we put Him first. That we obey and serve Him. That we allow Him to develop our character. Material provision *will* be given to us. That's the easiest thing in the world for the Owner of the universe to do.

## Don't Worry About Tomorrow's Troubles Today

"Therefore do not worry about tomorrow, for tomorrow will worry about itself. Each day has enough trouble of its own" (Matt. 6:34). When Jesus spoke these profound words, He didn't mean we would not experience heartache, pain, uncertainty, and suffering of all kinds. He simply meant we should not anticipate it ahead of time.

In other words, "Never borrow from the future. If you live in dread of what may happen and it doesn't happen, you have worried in vain. Even if it does happen, you have to worry twice. Worry is the interest paid to those who borrow trouble."[1]

You wouldn't try to reach the top of a flight of stairs by taking one giant leap from the bottom to the top, would you? No, you would climb one step at a time until you reached the top. In the same sense, God wants you to do what you can do today and leave the troubles of tomorrow for tomorrow's strength.

For one thing, 95 percent of the things we worry about never happen. Furthermore, as Corrie ten Boom wisely said, "Worry does not empty tomorrow of its sorrow; it empties today of its strength."

## Steps toward Freedom from Worry

Not only is worry counterproductive, it is also a form of disobedience. God has told us not to worry, so to worry is to disregard His guidance. Isn't it strange that we don't usually think of worry as sin? But it is! Confess it as sin. Choose with your will to obey God and depend on Him for the ability. Then consider the following suggestions (some of which are adapted from the book *Worry-Free Living* to help break the very self-destructive habit of worrying.[2]

## Meditate on God's Word Daily

Plan a time daily when you can spend some time—even if it's only fifteen minutes—reading the Bible. Think about what you read, and go over the phrases. Put your name in place of the pronouns, applying each verse to specific situations in your life. Memorize passages that will help you. God's Word is powerful—it will renew and protect your mind.

## Condition Yourself to Relax

Choose a phrase from Scripture or a hymn that you can repeat to yourself at the first hint of anxiety. "Tell it to Jesus" or "God cares for me" or "The Lord is my Shepherd, I shall not want." As you repeat the phrase, you will encourage yourself with its message and remind yourself to relax.

## Listen to Soothing Music

Just as David's music on the harp soothed King Saul's anxiety and depression, hymns and spiritual songs are wonderful tranquilizers for us today. Haven't you had the experience of hearing or singing a hymn that lifted your spirits and eased your mind? You might want to listen to a recording, play an instrument, or sing yourself. Reflect on the words and relax in the melody.

## Talk through Your Problems

When you are worried about an issue or a relationship, don't fail to communicate. If you need to talk with your husband, schedule a time when you can honestly tell him your concerns and listen to what he says. If it's necessary, talk with your supervisor or employer about some troublesome aspect of your job. Talk with your children and listen to them as well. Worries expand into giant problems when they are left in your imagination. They need to be exposed, then whittled down to size.

## Limit Your Worry Time

Counselors suggest this technique for people who are prone to anxiety: Set aside fifteen minutes a day for active worry—and no more. This will keep worry from distracting you for the rest of the day. If worrisome things come to mind, jot them down on a card and plan to think about them later. There are three positive results from this.

First, you can accomplish a great deal more during the day when you are free from anxiety.

Second, when your "worry time" comes, you're better able to deal with the problems because you feel good about your productive day. You can devote your total attention to your concerns and list them in order of seriousness.

Third, by the time you get to the worries, the problems may well have shrunk in importance. They may not seem worth worrying about after all.

## Design a Plan of Action

Suppose it's your child you're worried about. Do everything you can to protect him or her. Always have a reliable person care for your child when you aren't there. Teach your child to tell you if anyone touches his or her private parts. Warn the child never to go with strangers. Teach him or her a password that everyone must say. Do everything you can, then commit your child to the Lord for His protection.

Perhaps the thought of inviting people to dinner fills you with anxiety. You have a couple of options: You can refuse to entertain, or you can try to entertain and make yourself sick with worry in the process. Better yet, plan a menu you can prepare ahead of time. Arrange for the kids to spend the night with a friend in a trade-off. Clean your house ahead of time except for surface things. Rest an hour before your guests arrive. Then put everything together and enjoy your guests. Instead of worrying about a perfect performance, focus your attention on building relationships.

## Cultivate the Awareness of God's Presence in You

Jesus has promised never to leave us or forsake us. He is in us in the person of His Holy Spirit. He wants to live out His life through us. He gives us the strength for our tasks, the wisdom for decisions, the courage to face difficulties, and the victory over temptation. Keep up a running conversation with Him in your mind.

## Replace Worry with Prayer

Paul gave the Philippians some excellent advice about worrying when he wrote, "Do not be anxious about anything, but in everything, by prayer and petition, with thanksgiving, present your requests to God. And the peace of God, which transcends all understanding, will guard your hearts and your minds in Christ Jesus" (Phil. 4:6–7).

Instead of worrying, pray. You have a Father in heaven who is real, who loves you, who will provide for your every need. He wants you to pray, demonstrating your dependence on Him. And He will give you an unexplainable peace that will serve as a guardian over your mind.

As Peter instructed, "Cast all your anxiety on him

*worry*

because he cares for you" (1 Pet. 5:7). This is such a practical verse. "When something is on your mind that fills you with anxiety, write it down on a card. Hold the card up to the Lord for Him to read. Then say, "Lord, I'm casting this care on You for You to handle." Write across your worry, "I cast this on the Lord." And whenever an anxious thought sneaks back into your mind, say out loud, "That problem belongs to Jesus. I threw it on His shoulders." Keep the cards to remind you of your commitment, then go over them in a year's time. It will encourage you to see just how the Lord took care of each of your worries.

## Get Help from Others

Many times when I share with a friend something that is troubling me, I feel better immediately. Often my friend has wisdom from her own experience or from Scripture that encourages and enlightens me. We pray together, and by the time we part, God has used another believer to relieve my anxiety and strengthen my faith. Remember, we are members of one body, one family, and we are commanded to bear one another's burdens.

If you are a worrier, God wants to heal you. He has given you His promises, His protection, and His provision. We all have a choice. We can keep worrying, ruin our mental and physical health, and retard our spiritual development. Or we can cast our cares on the strong shoulders of our loving Savior who has promised to give us His peace.

# 7

~∞~

# A Disease Called Unforgiveness

WHEN I ASKED CHRISTINE how she felt about her parents, her attractive face seemed to lose all expression. She reflected for a moment, then matter-of-factly stated, "I get along fine with my parents. I just haven't seen them in a while. Why?"

I studied her, noticing that her large, blue eyes weren't looking into mine. They were fixed, instead, upon her slender fingers.

Christine had already told me that her father and mother had been rather cruel to her during her childhood. They had locked her in a closet when she didn't please them and had slapped her across the face repeatedly if she questioned their authority. Unfortunately, they were very active in their church and felt that they were disciplining her in a godly way. "If I break your will," her father had once told her, "then God won't have to."

Christine had moved out of the house at sixteen and had quickly created a life of her own. For many years, she'd wanted nothing to do with her father, mother, or their religion. More recently, however, her personal failures had reminded her that she needed a Savior. Grateful to learn that He wasn't the terrible God of her childhood, she had trusted Christ.

In response to her "Why?" question, I explained, "Well, you say you've got a short fuse and that you lose your temper more often than you'd like to. I was just wondering if you're still angry with your parents."

"My parents did the best they could," she answered coolly. "They thought strictness was the biblical way to bring me up. They never meant to hurt me."

"I don't agree," I explained. "I don't think they did the best they could do. Child abuse is sin, and they sinned against you."

"Well, I'm supposed to forgive them, right? So that's my way of forgiving them—I'm willing to say they did the best they could. And I just avoid seeing them as much as possible."

"That's not forgiveness, Christine. Forgiveness is acknowledging everything they did to you. You need to face the fact that they treated you very, very badly. Then, with God's help, you can forgive them for the worst things they ever did. Watering it all down and then walking away from it is not forgiveness."

Christine and I discussed at length the cold, hard facts about her childhood. She prayed that God would forgive her parents for several specific incidents when they deeply wounded her physically, emotionally, and spiritually. In the months to come, Christine found that her unwelcome rage and short temper were diminishing. Through improved communication and honesty, she was eventually able to establish a comfortable adult relationship with both her father and her mother.

## Forgiveness—A Challenging Requirement

"To err is human, to forgive, divine." When Alexander Pope wrote those immortal words, he stated a truth that still resonates in our own hearts. Forgiving others seems to be one of the hardest things some of us ever have to do. Why?

At times it is difficult to face the wrongs that have been done to us. Like Christine, we deny, even to ourselves, the severity of our wounds.

In other cases, we are well aware of the hurts we've experienced, and we believe the offender should suffer some consequences for what he or she did. If we forgive, it seems we're letting the culprit off too easily. We don't want to encourage repeated offenses.

Then there's the element of trust. Our trust is eroded with each hurtful incident. Isn't it wise simply to write the person off or to avoid him or her as much as possible? That way we can protect ourselves from the possibility of further pain.

Like Christine, you may carry the memory of offenses that date all the way back to your childhood years. Your parents may have rejected you or abused you. Perhaps your mother preferred your sister because she was attractive and you were not. Or maybe your father made it his habit to hit you first and ask questions later.

You might be in a marriage that requires you to forgive almost daily, even though all feelings of love and warmth have disappeared.

And let's not forget the injustices you may have experienced in the workplace—passed over for a position just because you are a woman or because you wouldn't go to bed with the boss.

Life offers us plenty of opportunities to feel unforgiving. The trouble is, lack of forgiveness does more damage to us than to the offender. When we don't forgive, we grow hardened, untrusting, sour, and bitter. We become vengeful. We want the person who wronged us to suffer. Those negative feelings war against the love and compassion that should characterize us as Christians, and we hinder our own spiritual growth.

God knows how difficult forgiving is for us to do. And His Word records—in great detail—the life of a man who had more to forgive than almost anyone. We learn valuable lessons about forgiveness from Joseph, whose story is told in the book of Genesis.

## Israel's Favorite Son

Joseph was not to blame for his misfortunes. Jacob, his father, provoked Joseph's abuse through his open favoritism. Joseph was Jacob's favorite child because he was the son of Rachel, the wife Jacob loved the most dearly. And Joseph's ten half-brothers were well aware of it. You'd think Jacob would have remembered all the problems that transpired in his own family due to favoritism. But he was like many parents today: Tragically, we are prone to repeat the sins of our parents rather than to learn from them.

"Now Israel loved Joseph more than any of his other sons, because he had been born to him in his old age; and he made a richly ornamented robe for him. When his brothers saw that their father loved him more than any of them, they hated him and could not speak a kind word to him" (Gen. 37:3–4).

Joseph's brothers already hated him. It just made matters worse when he dreamed two strange dreams, both predicting his rise to prominence and authority, indicating that he would rule over his family. That was more than his brothers could take. We read, "They hated him all the more because of his dream" (Gen. 37:8).

More than once, the ten half-brothers must have discussed how great it would be to get rid of Joseph. Finally, one day he walked into their clutches, and they had their opportunity. They threw him into a pit and tried to figure out how to snuff out his life. Just then a caravan of merchants passed by. Instead of murdering him, they decided to sell Joseph to the slave traders, who took him to Egypt.

## Painful Circumstances, Painful Memories

We can only imagine Joseph's thoughts as he trudged through the desert on his way to Egypt. As he slept every night in the slave quarters. As he was ordered to do menial tasks day after day—tasks his father's servants did at home. Poor Joseph must have been devastated by the rejection and hatred of his brothers. He surely longed for his father's embrace. He could never have dreamed that his brothers' animosity would lead to this.

What kind of person would Joseph have become if he had nurtured an unforgiving spirit? We have to imagine such a thing, because Scripture gives us every evidence that he didn't let injustice erode his character or his trust in God. It didn't matter where he was, whether in the house of Potiphar, the captain of Pharaoh's guard, or chained in a prison cell on a false charge of rape, or sitting on a throne in Egypt—we read of God's favor upon Joseph: "The LORD was with Joseph and he prospered. . . . The LORD gave him success in everything he did. . . . The LORD was with him; he showed him kindness and granted him favor" (Gen. 39:2–3, 21).

Joseph was a slave. He was owned as property in an idolatrous, pagan country. Yet he never lost his awareness of the presence of the living God and his accountability to Him. Again and again, he spoke fearlessly of his God to Egyptians of every rank, always sprinkling his answers to their various questions and charges with references to his heavenly Father:

- "How then could I do such a wicked thing and sin against God?" (39:9).

- "Do not interpretations belong to God?" (40:8).

- "I cannot do it, but God will give Pharaoh the answer he desires" (41:16).

- "God has revealed to Pharaoh what he is about to do" (41:25).

- "The matter has been firmly decided by God and God will do it soon" (41:32).

## The Right Man to Know in Egypt

Joseph did not wallow in self-pity or allow himself to be eaten alive by bitterness. He never planned ways to avenge himself against his wicked brothers. If he had done so, he could never have retained such a close relationship with God. Instead, Joseph accepted what had happened to him, and in doing so, he was able to mature in his faith. At last the day came when he had his chance—he could choose to exact revenge or he could decide to demonstrate forgiveness.

God had revealed, through Pharaoh's dreams, that seven years of abundant harvests in Egypt would be followed by seven years of drought and famine. When Joseph interpreted the dreams, Pharaoh placed him, a thirty-year-old, in charge of all the food in Egypt. Joseph built storehouses for grain throughout the land during the years of plenty. Then, when the years of famine ravaged Egypt and the surrounding countries, he was also in charge of selling grain.

One day, his heart leaped within him. To his amazement, he recognized the men bowing before him, in search of food, as his own brothers! Joseph had forgiven these men long before, but he had some questions that needed answers before he let them know who he was.

Were they still the same vicious thugs who had treated him so heartlessly?

Did they feel any remorse for what they had done?

Had they done anything to harm his only full brother, Benjamin?

Was his father alive or had grief killed him?

Joseph tested them in various ingenious ways to find the answers. He listened as they expressed their guilt to each other in their own language. He ordered them to bring Benjamin to Egypt so he could see for himself that he was alive and well. He verified for himself that they weren't jealous of Benjamin as they had been of him—one brother, Judah, even offered himself as a hostage in Benjamin's place rather than bringing further grief to their father by taking Benjamin away from home.

Twenty-two years earlier, these same men hadn't even considered their father's feelings when they brought Joseph's torn and bloody coat and threw it at Jacob's feet. Yes, they had changed. Joseph was convinced he could trust them.

## Learning from Joseph's Example

Take a few moments and read Genesis 45. Here Joseph reveals his true identity to his family, and they respond. As he did so, Joseph demonstrated for us some important principles about forgiveness:

## Give Up the Need for Revenge

A craving for revenge is very normal. However, it is a negative emotion that doesn't hurt the other person unless we actually carry it out. Meanwhile, it can control and corrupt us.

While we spend time fantasizing about ways to strike back, we remain in emotional turmoil, frustrated and unhappy. It's a healthy and necessary step to give up the need for retaliation. We who know the Lord have a Defender. We can commit our cause into His hands and let Him be the One who does what is just. As the psalmist wrote, "But you, O God, do see trouble and grief; you consider it to take it in hand. The victim commits himself to you" (Ps. 10:14–15).

Jesus set our example for forgiveness when He hung on the cross. "When they hurled their insults at him, he did not retaliate; when he suffered, he made no threats. Instead, he entrusted himself to him who judges justly" (1 Pet. 2:23).

We can give up the need to retaliate because we can commit our cause to our heavenly Father. He is a Judge who will not let the guilty go free. Joseph would not have become the man he was if he had spent thirteen years of hardship in Egypt plotting revenge . . . and that brings us to the next aspect of forgiveness.

## Don't Absolve the Guilty Party of Responsibility

We shouldn't try to pretend that nothing hurtful has happened when it has. As Joseph's brothers stood before him, begging for his help, he told them, "I am your brother whom you sold into Egypt." You shouldn't simply forget that your father or stepfather raped you as a child. You shouldn't disregard the fact that your mother neglected or abandoned you. You shouldn't pretend that your husband didn't have several affairs.

The trouble with *forgetting* is that it grants absolution. It is also a form of denial: "If I forgive you, we can pretend that what happened wasn't so terrible."

This kind of forgetting keeps you from expressing your emotions. So how can you acknowledge your anger against a person you have already forgiven? As Susan Forward suggests, "Responsibility can only go to one of two places: outward, onto the people who have hurt you, or inward, into yourself. So you may forgive the other person but end up hating yourself all the more in exchange."[1]

We need to admit feeling the emotions that painful events have aroused. If we don't acknowledge them, we will never deal with them, and they will control our lives. Instead, we need to place the responsibility on the individuals who deserve it. And even though we forgive, we also have a right to determine if they have changed before we trust them in the future.

Sometimes a woman tells me her husband has been physically abusive in the past. Each time he says he's sorry and won't do it again, so she forgives him. Then he does it again. Each time she finds it harder to forgive because she trusts him less. But then *she* feels guilty for not forgiving and forgetting.

In fact, *he* is the one who has violated her trust and not earned it back, because he hasn't changed. He is the one who must be held responsible for his behavior. There are consequences for our sins. God forgives our sins but we usually suffer the temporal consequences. An abused wife's lack of trust is a consequence for her husband's sins. Joseph was very careful to determine what his brothers were like before he decided to trust them.

Sometimes we don't have the opportunity to regain trust. One woman told me that her father had molested her when she was a teenager. By the time she and I had our conversation, she was in her forties, and she still had not forgiven him. The thing that infuriated her was that she could never confront him and get an apology—because he had been dead for several years! In this woman's case, she had to forgive her father, apology or no apology, because the bitterness that was consuming her was corrosive to her own spirit. We *must* forgive, if only for the sake of our own spiritual health.

## One Goal of Forgiveness Is Reconciliation

When Joseph finally revealed his identity to his brothers, they wept together, embraced, and kissed. Then he told them to bring their father and all their families to Egypt, where he could provide for them during the years of famine. Thus Joseph was reunited with his family after twenty-two years of separation.

Can you imagine what that meant to all of them, especially to Jacob? Reconciliation is one of the primary purposes for forgiving. It doesn't always happen, of course, depending on the circumstances, but it should be an ultimate goal.

Jesus stressed the importance of reconciliation when He taught, "If your brother sins against you, go and show him his fault, just between the two of you. If he listens to you, you have won your brother over. But if he will not listen, take one or two others along, so that 'every matter may be established by the testimony of two or three witnesses'" (Matt. 18:15–17).

Don't hold a grudge. Instead, approach the one who has hurt you so that you may be reconciled. If he refuses, it's a matter for church discipline—something we don't practice very much today.

The reason for this policy is that when family members are estranged it affects the whole family. Likewise, when members of God's family are estranged, it affects the local church. It hinders the work of the Holy Spirit who wants the whole body to grow to maturity in Christ.

Another time Jesus urged His followers to be ready to forgive each other over and over again, if necessary. When Peter asked, "Lord, how many times shall I forgive my brother when he sins against me? Up to seven times?" Jesus answered, "I tell you, not seven times, but seventy-seven times" (Matt. 18:21–22).

Peter had some trouble understanding how many times he should forgive. Jewish tradition said three times, so Peter thought he was being really generous when he picked the perfect number, seven. What a shock Jesus' answer was! The King James Version says, "seventy times seven"—in other words, a number without limit!

## Forgiveness Is Free to the Offender but Costly to the Forgiver

Jesus used a parable to give us God's perspective about forgiveness. He described a king who forgave his servant's massive debt—it amounted to what would be millions of dollars today. But the servant turned right around and refused to forgive a fellow servant's debt of around ten dollars. When the king heard about it, he was enraged. He sent the servant he had forgiven to the torturers in the prison. "This is how my heavenly Father will treat each of you," Jesus explained, "unless you forgive your brother from your heart" (Matt. 18:35).

In Jesus' story, the king freely forgave his servant, but he absorbed the cost. In the same way, God forgave us, but He absorbed the debt of our sin when Christ died on the cross in our place. Like Him, we are to give forgiveness freely to the sinner, even though it is costly to us.

## We Must Forgive Because God Forgave Us

If we have trusted Christ, we have been freely forgiven for every sin we have ever committed or ever will commit. For this reason we are to freely forgive others. The king forgave the servant's debt of millions of dollars, yet the forgiven servant would not forgive a debt of ten dollars. God views our lack of forgiveness for one another from the same perspective. His Word urges us to "Get rid of all bitterness, rage and anger, brawling and slander, along with every form of malice. Be kind and compassionate to one another, forgiving each other, just as in Christ God forgave you" (Eph. 4:31–32).

It takes a major effort of the will to "forgive each other, just as in Christ God forgave you" because most of the time, we don't feel like forgiving. The first step we have to take to do this is to tell the Lord that even though we don't want to do it, even though we aren't willing to do it, we *are* willing for Him to make us willing. When we choose with our will to obey God, He will give us the power to do what is necessary.

## Believe That God Will Use Your Pain to Accomplish His Purpose for Your Life

Years after their father, Jacob, had died, the brothers still could not believe Joseph had really forgiven them, because they had never forgiven themselves. "When Joseph's brothers saw that their father was dead, they said, 'What if Joseph holds a grudge against us and pays us back for all the wrongs we did to him?'" (Gen. 50:15).

Joseph's answer gives us the right perspective: "Don't be afraid. Am I in the place of God? You intended to harm me, but God intended it for good to accomplish what is now being done, the saving of many lives" (Gen. 50:19–21).

Joseph still placed the responsibility for their actions on them, but he had no desire to avenge himself. He knew what we should remember: God is the only righteous Judge.

God is Sovereign. He doesn't abdicate His Sovereignty when someone treats us unjustly. Instead, He weaves the dark threads of pain into the tapestry of our lives to deepen our character and accomplish his purpose. As Philip Yancey has said, "Faith believes ahead of time what can only be seen by looking back."

Can you look back on your life and see now how God has used painful experiences to shape your character? How He has provided opportunities and understanding you never would have had without your suffering? If there's someone you have difficulty forgiving, you can safely believe that God will use the experience to accomplish His purpose in your life. Commit your cause to Him, and let Him do what is right. Justice may not happen here on earth, but it will happen someday.

## Forgiveness Is Something Good You Do for Yourself

God, in His grace, has forgiven us a debt we can never repay. His generosity to us is the basis for our forgiveness of others. We're told, "See to it that no one misses the grace of God and that no bitter root grows up to cause trouble and defile many" (Heb. 12:15).

If we won't forgive, bitterness will become firmly entrenched in our characters. It will make us cynical, unable to trust, and unable to maintain close relationships. Just as in Jesus' parable of the unforgiving servant who was sent to the torturers, our own bitterness will torture us for a lifetime. On the other hand, forgiveness will free us to go on in peace, unhindered in our enjoyment of the Lord. Let's forgive. Let's let go of the past and leave all the paying back to Him.

# 8

## The Truth about Anger

WHEN JERRI CAME TO SEE ME in my office, I was delighted for a chance to talk to her again. She had been a part of our women's Bible study for several years, and I had always liked her personally. During earlier counseling sessions she had talked to me about her past, and I'd been shocked by the number of deep heartbreaks she had encountered. Now I watched her move slowly to a chair, sit down, and fold her hands limply in her lap.

I remembered that, as a child, Jerri had been sexually molested by an uncle. Then, after twenty years of marriage, her husband had left her for another woman. Her teenage son had gone to live with him, and the son and ex-husband had recently moved to another state, leaving her childless and rejected. Now, as we talked, I learned that a man she had been dating had abruptly broken up with her and was seeing a girl in her twenties. The years had not been kind to Jerri— she hadn't managed to retain a youthful appearance. A recent series of physical ailments had left her pale and thin. And the loss of her romance clearly hadn't helped matters either. Tremendous sadness reflected from her eyes. Jerri quickly admitted that she was struggling with depression. My heart went out to her, and I felt a surge of indignation toward the many people who had treated her so unkindly.

"It's amazing, Jerri, after all you've been through, that you have such a calm manner. Don't you feel angry?"

Jerri smiled sweetly. "Oh, no! We were taught as children never to be angry. As you know, anger is a sin. I don't want to lose God's approval by getting mad at somebody who's hurt me. God is all I have left," she concluded sadly.

I shook my head and corrected her. "Anger is *not* a sin, Jerri, and you're not going to jeopardize your relationship with God by feeling angry. He gets angry too. Of course we sometimes do sinful things when we're upset, but anger itself is an emotion, not a sin. You're bound to be angry after all that's happened. But instead of allowing yourself to feel your anger and instead of directing it toward the people who deserve it, you're stuffing it inside yourself. You're turning your anger inward, on yourself. No wonder you're so depressed!

Like many Christians, Jerri was operating under the misconception that anger is always "bad." And her refusal to accept her anger was adversely affecting her life. As Les Carter writes, "Anger per se is neither good nor bad. It is how people use their anger that makes it positive or negative. Ideally, anger was given to humans by God as a tool to help build relationships. In its pure form anger is an emotional signal that tells a person something needs to be changed. It was intended to be a positive motivator to be used in giving one another feedback about how life can be lived more productively"[1]

If all anger were wrong, we wouldn't find the many references to God's anger in the Old Testament. There are approximately 365 references to God's anger and 80 references to man's. Since God is holy, we must understand His anger as his righteous response to human sin and rebellion. Yet over and over we also read that God is "compassionate and gracious, slow to anger, abounding in love, and forgiving wickedness, rebellion and sin" (Exod. 34:6–7).

## Jesus and Anger

In the New Testament, there are several words used most frequently to express anger.

- *Thumos* appears twenty times and means a turbulent commotion, boiling agitation of feeling, sudden explosion. It's like our word *rage*.

- *Orge* appears forty-five times and describes a long-lasting attitude that often continues to seek revenge, like our word *resentment*.

- *Aganaktesis*, mentioned five times, is a form of anger without the implication of inappropriate behavior: *indignation*.[2]

In the New Testament, Jesus teaches us some of the things that anger God. Jesus acted out His anger when He drove the moneychangers out of the temple courts. He did this because they had made God's house a marketplace; they had cheated people and prevented them from worshiping God (see Matt. 21:12).

He became angry with the Pharisees because of their heartlessness. They wanted Him to keep the rules they had made for the Sabbath, and they had no compassion for the man with the shriveled hand whom Jesus healed (see Mark 3:5).

Jesus was very indignant when the disciples tried to prevent people from bringing children to Him (see Mark 10:14).

He consistently felt "righteous anger toward oppression, injustice, and unmet human needs. And he didn't hesitate to express his angry feelings."[3] Since Jesus was without sin, He vividly demonstrated for us that all anger is *not* sin.

## Anger—Good or Bad

Rage expresses anger in explosive words and/or actions. Resentment stuffs the anger inside. Both forms of anger can destroy our relationships, affect our personalities, damage our effectiveness, and color our sense of worth. Indignation, however, can be the motivation for constructive action.

Where would we be today if God-fearing men and women had not become indignant about the terrible traffic in slaves that dehumanized black people?

Florence Nightingale's indignation over the unsanitary conditions and terrible care British soldiers received when they were wounded in battle revolutionized the nursing profession.

Dr. Semelweiss's indignation over the high mortality rate of mothers in childbirth led to the sterile procedures that save so many lives today.

The indignation we feel at the slaughter of millions of unborn infants has generated the pro-life movement. We have seen how this protest can be done in a manner consistent with Christianity. We have also seen how it can lead to sin, such as the murder of abortionists.

More and more people, even non-Christians, are expressing indignation at the filth on TV and in the movies.

Indignation over the abuse of women and children has caused people to take action. Concerned men and women have created shelters to protect the victims of domestic violence and develop programs to help the batterers.

Indignation stirs us to action. It starts our engines. God has given us this emotion as a tool to protest evil, to mobilize us to action, to correct injustice, and to give us a passion for service. When we are angry about the things that anger God, we are on a safe track.

Moses exhibited righteous indignation when he came down from Mount Sinai after forty days of talking with God and receiving his holy law. At the foot of the mountain, he found the Israelites in a wild orgy, dancing around a golden calf. He smashed the two tablets of stone to the ground, shattering them as powerfully as their laws had been shattered by the people's rebellion. God did not rebuke him for that.

But forty years later, Moses' rash, impatient anger exploded in rage, and he disobeyed God and struck a rock twice with his staff instead of speaking to it as God had commanded. For this display of anger, Moses was rebuked by God and forbidden to enter the Promised Land.

## What Makes You Angry?

We can learn a great deal about ourselves by considering the kinds of things that make us angry. Ask yourself the following questions, and try to be honest in your responses.

- Does your husband make you angry because he doesn't pick up his dirty clothes when the hamper is just six steps away?

- Are you resentful toward your mother-in-law because she interferes or keeps competing for first place with your husband?

- Do you feel indignation when a fellow employee is treated unfairly?

- Do the men at work anger you with their comments, jokes, and put-downs about women?

- Do you get irritated with your boyfriend because he is not as attentive as you would like?

- Do you respond with anger when your children are difficult to handle or disobedient?

- Does it upset you when your husband doesn't really listen to what you are trying to tell him?

- Are you resentful toward your boss because he is demanding and unsympathetic about your family pressures?

- Do you get angry when you seem to lose control over others?

- Are you enraged when your pride is bruised?

- Is your anger the result of ongoing grudges and bitterness?

- What is your emotional response to irritations? Do you blow up at the least provocation then forget the incident and leave the debris of injury in your wake?

- Do you suppress your anger and nurse a growing pile of offenses that keep you seething inside, while on the outside you pretend that you're okay?

# The Truth about Anger

• Is your anger an impetus for producing change?

Considering your answers to these questions can help you reflect upon the sources of your anger.

## Anger Management—God's Way

You probably noticed that God's Word doesn't say we will never be angry. Nor does it say that all anger is sin. However, it does set limits for us. We're told, "In your anger do not sin: Do not let the sun go down while you are still angry, and do not give the devil a foothold" (Eph. 4:26–27).

Anger can be a constructive tool, able to build bridges, not walls, if it's managed properly. For example, if we commit ourselves to dealing with our anger before we go to bed, it won't grow during the night into resentment and bitterness. Dealing with anger before bedtime is not always an easy thing to do because at times there's no way of confronting the other person on the day of the incident. In that case, we have to take the circumstances to the Lord and promise Him we will work out the details as soon as possible. Otherwise, we are warned that unresolved anger gives the devil a foothold in our lives.

Anger is a wedge the devil drives into our spirits. If it's unresolved, it can lead to discouragement, depression, hatred, and even murder. It can cause friction and divisiveness in a family, a church, or in the workplace. That's why Scripture advises us, "Do not let any unwholesome talk come out of your mouths, but only what is helpful for building others up according to their needs, that it may benefit those who listen. And do not grieve the Holy Spirit of God, with whom you were sealed for the day of redemption" (Eph. 4:29–32).

When we speak unkindly or negatively, we grieve the Holy Spirit who lives within us. Why does He grieve? Because even though He is willing to give us the power to react differently, we choose to ignore Him. He is there to radiate Christ through our bodies, and we persist in snuffing out that light with our sins. Although these behaviors are the products of our sinful natures, we no longer have to be under their control.

In the New Testament, particularly in Galatians 5:16–26, we learn that there are two sources of power for our lives: The sinful nature and the Holy Spirit. The sinful nature was crucified with Christ. Its control over us was broken. Now we have Christ Himself living His life in us.

When we follow the Holy Spirit's guidance, yield our emotions to His control, and are attentive to His gentle nudges, He will produce in us the character of Jesus Christ: "love, joy, peace, patience, kindness, goodness, faithfulness, gentleness and self-control" (Gal. 5:22). If these qualities are deeply ingrained in our character, they will surely change the way we respond to irritation and provocation.

## Two Ways to Express Anger

Psychologists today have classified the way we handle our anger into two categories: *assertive* and *aggressive*.

In his book *Good 'n' Angry*, Les Carter distinguishes the two: "Assertive anger puts forward one's beliefs and values in a confident, self-assured manner. It is helpful and considerate of others. When used correctly, assertiveness is a positive trait. Assertive anger seeks to put forward what a person believes to be right. However, aggressive anger is used in an abrasive, insensitive way. . . . There is little concern for the impact the anger will have on the recipient. Aggressive anger is a negative trait."[4]

An incident in the life of the biblical character Nehemiah allows us to see how he dealt with a situation that made him very angry. He is a good example of an individual who used his anger assertively, and his restraint produced positive results.

Nehemiah was in the midst of accomplishing a great work. He had returned to Jerusalem from an influential position in the court of Babylon, and he had traveled there for one purpose: to organize the disheartened Jews living in Jerusalem to rebuild the walls around the city. Everybody was working day and night to finish the job. Then a delegation of poor Jews came to him with a complaint:

"Now the men and their wives raised a great outcry against their Jewish brothers. Some were saying, 'We and our sons and daughters are numerous; in order for us to eat and stay alive, we must get grain.'

"Others were saying, 'We are mortgaging our fields, our vineyards and our homes to get grain during the famine.'

"Still others were saying, 'We have had to borrow money to pay the king's tax on our fields and vineyards. Although we are of the same flesh and blood as our countrymen and though our sons are as good as theirs, yet we have to subject our sons and daughters to slavery. Some of our daughters have already been enslaved, but we are powerless, because our fields and our vineyards belong to others'" (Neh. 5:1–5).

Wealthy Jews were taking advantage of their poor brothers by lending them money and demanding interest and collateral. This was in direct violation of the Mosaic law—Jews were never to charge interest to their own poor.

Furthermore, they were forbidden to enslave another Jew for any reason. A debtor could work off his debt as a hired hand.

Nehemiah 5:6 records Nehemiah's response: "When I heard their outcry and these charges, I was very angry."

Nehemiah's reaction was one of indignation—righteous indignation, and his anger was in sync with God's anger.

How can we use anger to bring about change? Here are some valuable principles about anger we can learn from Nehemiah:

### Admit Feeling Angry

Nehemiah never covered up his emotions. He acknowledged them openly and without apology. His anger started his engines and motivated him to action.

### Think Before You Speak

Nehemiah didn't spout off the first thing that came into his head. He said, "I pondered them in my mind and then accused the nobles and officials" (Neh. 5:7a).

Have you ever spouted off and then been sorry afterward? Words that pop out of our mouths in the heat of anger are usually things we would not say if we thought about them first. Nehemiah controlled his tongue until he had "pondered." He planned exactly what he would do and demand.

The New Testament gives us similar instructions: "Everyone should be quick to listen, slow to speak and slow to become angry, for man's anger does not bring about the righteous life that God desires" (James 1:19–20).

### Confront and Propose a Solution

Once he'd thought things through, Nehemiah spoke: "I told them, 'You are exacting usury from your own countrymen!' So I called together a large meeting to deal with them and said . . .

"'What you are doing is not right. Shouldn't you walk in the fear of our God to avoid the reproach of our Gentile enemies? I and my brothers and my men are also lending the people money and grain. But let the exacting of usury stop! Give back to them immediately their fields, vineyards, olive groves and houses, and also the usury you are charging them—the hundredth part of the money, grain, new wine and oil'" (Neh. 5:7b, 9–11).

Nehemiah knew that he had scriptural support for his point of view, so he was fearless as he confronted these influential men—he charged them with violating God's laws.

Sometimes we treat people of wealth and power in a different way, giving them more preferential treatment than we do those who have none. We do this because we don't want to rock the boat. We don't want to lose their contributions. We don't want them to retaliate. We don't want a lawsuit.

But not Nehemiah! He didn't mince any words. He said, "What you are doing is wrong! Stop it! Give back what you've taken!" He stood uncompromisingly for justice. His own example put them to shame. He demanded immediate restitution. He didn't allow for any halfway measures. And what was the response from these powerful men?

"'We will give it back,' they said. 'And we will not demand anything more from them. We will do as you say.'"

Then Nehemiah made sure they wouldn't backslide. "I summoned the priests and made the nobles and officials take an oath to do what they had promised. I also shook out the folds of my robe and said, 'In this way may God shake out of his house and possessions every man who does not keep this promise. So may such a man be shaken out and emptied!'

"At this the whole assembly said, 'Amen,' and praised the LORD. And the people did as they had promised" (Neh. 5: 12–13).

Nehemiah had no illusions about people. He was wise enough to make these men take an oath in public, before the Lord, that they would do as they promised. He threatened them with God's punishment if they reneged on their promises. And they all followed through. Nehemiah's indignation resulted in restitution and justice for his oppressed countrymen.

## Check Your Stress Level

I find that when I haven't had enough sleep or I'm under a lot of stress that I have a tendency to say things I don't mean and speak in a tone of voice I wouldn't normally use. When you find yourself getting angry, check your stress level to see if you aren't tired, impatient, and oversensitive.

## Danger in the Hormone Zone

Normal hormonal changes can also play a part in our tolerance level. When I was in the midst of menopause, my middle son was entering puberty. I realized I was irritable and often unreasonable in my dealings with him during a time when he, too, was experiencing unfamiliar feelings and fears. At times we seemed like hostile strangers rather than loving mother and son. To say the least, we were a poorly matched pair.

One day, I sat down with him and said, "Robert, you've reached a time of your life when your body is changing. You are becoming a man, and you'll soon be able to reproduce children. And I'm at the opposite end of the spectrum—my body is losing the ability to have babies. Both of us are experiencing feelings we haven't had before. If you help me, we can get through this together with a lot less difficulty."

Since I seemed to have his full attention, I went on. "Robert, there are two things that really bother me, clutter and noise. Do you think you could be more orderly and less noisy?" My explanation helped him to understand. He was so sweet and responsive. After that conversation, he really made an effort to be considerate, and I tried to be more tolerant. This got both of us through a tough period.

## Yield Your Temper to the Control of the Holy Spirit

The Holy Spirit lives within us and wants us to have victory over our besetting sins. He is the one who produces self-control in us. The more we let Him take over, the more self-control we will have. This begins with a "time-out" process.

In order to keep our temper from controlling us, we have to take time out to turn our minds toward God. We have to choose to offer up our circumstances to Him, to release the outcome to Him, and to ask Him for guidance and wisdom.

## Resist Satan and the Spirit of Anger

We need to resist Satan every morning *before* we encounter the situations that trigger anger in you. As James instructed us, "Submit yourselves, then, to God. Resist the devil and he will flee from you" (James 4:7).

## Choose to Forgive

As we learned in the last chapter, choosing to forgive is an act of the will. And a big difference in our behavior occurs when we live our lives knowing we are *always* going to forgive instead of giving ourselves permission to hold grudges.

## Accept Your Circumstances from God—They May Not Change

If you find that you are continually made angry by your circumstances, chances are you are waiting for God to do something miraculous. Maybe you're waiting for Him to change your world into a better place. The fact is, He is more likely to change *you*—from the inside out—so that you are able to cope with your present circumstances. In the meantime, He will use that difficult situation—perhaps it's your mate, child, parent, or employer—to develop the fruit of the Spirit in your life. In the meanwhile, "We also rejoice in our sufferings, because we know that suffering produces perseverance; perseverance, character; and character, hope. And hope does not disappoint us, because God has poured out his love into our hearts by the Holy Spirit, whom he has given us" (Rom. 5:3–4).

## If You Fail, Confess It As Sin Immediately

When losing your temper causes you to say or do something inappropriate, immediately take responsibility. First confess your failure to the Lord, and accept His forgiveness (see 1 John 1:9). Then go to the person you have offended and say those two difficult little words: "I'm sorry." Finally, go a little further and say, "What can we do to work this out?"

## Pray for Wisdom

Wisdom is one thing we can count on God to provide us with every time we ask. James 1:5 tells us that God delights in giving us wisdom. When we are faced with an infuriating situation, we need to pray for a constructive solution to the problem. This may entail a readjustment of our attitudes. It may require a compromise based on open communication. Most likely, the answer will come through hard work, not through an instantaneous change.

And when it comes to communication, pray that you are able to express your feelings in the right way and at the right time. Suppose you have to talk to your husband about something that bothers you a great deal. You know it won't be easy because he gets defensive and accusatory if you so much as broach the subject.

Pray about it. Then try bringing it up in a loving, peaceful way. You might want to approach him after a nice dinner in a quiet restaurant. Hold his hands. Look into his eyes and say, "I need to talk to you about something that is really troubling me. I need your help in working this out."

It is usually best to wait until you are feeling calm to explain why you have been angry. That way, even if he becomes irate, at least one of you will be thinking and speaking rationally!

Nehemiah's story makes one thing clear: All anger is not sin. Indignation motivates us to correct wrongs while rage and resentment keep us from maturing emotionally and growing spiritually. With the help of God's Spirit, we can learn to recognize the difference. Through His presence within, we will react His way to this challenging world—a world in which rage and violence are leaving horrifying scars at every level of society. We can be agents of change!

# 9

## Envy—The Green-Eyed Tyrant

HOLLY WAS A BRIGHT, PRETTY CHILD. But she had a peculiar habit—she always wanted her friends' toys. She cried when her best friend got a beautiful doll for her birthday. She whined when the neighbor girls appeared at church in matching Laura Ashley Easter dresses. She pouted when her sister was taken to Disney World as a reward for straight A's throughout high school.

When Holly became a teenager, she turned her attention toward boys. She quickly mastered the use of makeup, lightened her hair dramatically, and learned to dress with a slightly sexy flair. Her competitive drive always drew her toward her friends' boyfriends, and she made it her habit to call them, ask them for advice, and sow seeds of criticism about the girls in their lives. Then, at eighteen, she met Jack and Tammy Jensen, a couple in their thirties who were youth leaders at her church.

At first Holly innocently joined the other kids at the

Jensens' home. They gathered as a group, watched videos, and just hung out. But before long, Holly was spending a lot of time talking to Jack—alone. Like any married couple, Jack and Tammy had their small differences from time to time, and Holly instinctively homed in on them. While flattering Jack on one hand, on the other she gently questioned his reactions to Tammy's quick temper, her same old hairstyle, or her not-quite-perfect housekeeping.

Holly's divisive arts were astonishing, as were her manipulative capabilities. She called the Jensen home in tears one night from a pay phone, hysterically claiming to have been kicked out of the house by her parents. She asked Jack if he could pick her up. She knew the family well enough to calculate that Tammy would be getting dinner on the table for the children and that Jack would arrive alone. He did.

Jack listened to her story patiently, and by now he felt close enough to Holly to put his arms around her in comfort. The truth was, he'd been wanting to hold her in his arms for weeks. Before the night was over, the two of them had made love. Before the year was over, Jack and Tammy had filed for divorce, Jack had left the church, and he and Holly were living together.

The tragedy didn't end with the breakup of Jack and Holly's marriage. In fact it continues. Holly has become disillusioned with Jack—she complains that he's too old for her. She constantly compares him to younger men, humiliating him with caustic jokes about his weight, his thinning hair, and his middle-aged attitudes. Holly wants a house at the beach, like the Fosters'. She needs a new Chevy Suburban, like the Jarvises'. She and Jack fight constantly and bitterly over her insatiable desires for more things, better things, things her friends have that she'll never get because Jack is "such a boring old man."

## Jealousy and Envy—Good News, Bad News

Jealousy and envy are emotions we all feel from time to time. But if they are allowed to become dominant in our lives, they warp our perspectives, keep us from realizing our personal potential, and in cases like Holly's, lead us into destructive behavior. Without question, jealousy and envy impede our growth to spiritual maturity.

Although we sometimes use the words *jealousy* and *envy* interchangeably, there is a difference. Jealousy can be used in a good sense. Its root is *zelos,* the same word from which we also get *zeal,* or *zealous.* When the word is applied to God, saying He is a jealous God means He demands that we worship and love Him exclusively.

In a bad sense, jealousy is a fear of being displaced by a rival in affection or favor. To be jealous is to be anxiously suspicious or vigilant. Proverb 27:4 says, "Anger is cruel and fury overwhelming, but who can stand before jealousy?" The implication of this Scripture is that jealousy is hidden. It corrupts our motives, thoughts, and actions. To make matters worse, the object of that jealousy may be unaware of it and therefore be unable to deal with it.

While jealousy can be positive, envy, on the other hand, always has a bad meaning. Envy is defined as "a feeling of discontent and resentment aroused by another's desirable possessions or qualities, accompanied by a strong desire to have them for oneself."[1]

Scripture reminds us, "A heart at peace gives life to the body, but envy rots the bones" (Prov. 14:30).

## The Story of Rachel and Leah

In the Old Testament, we have classic examples of jealousy and envy in the lives of two women who were victims of their culture. Leah and Rachel were sisters, and they were married to the same man, Jacob. Have you noticed how many of our lessons have been centered on Jacob and his family? Talk about being dysfunctional!

In Genesis 5, Jacob was fleeing the wrath of his brother, Esau. When he reached Paddan-Aram, where his mother's family lived, his cousin Rachel was the first person he met. For him, their meeting was love at first sight. He was warmly welcomed into his Uncle Laban's home and began helping him shepherd his flocks.

Jacob asked Laban for Rachel's hand in marriage and volunteered to work seven years in return for her. Laban agreed, but then he deceived Jacob by secretly marrying him to his older, less attractive daughter, Leah. Laban agreed to give Rachel to Jacob, too, but he would have to work seven more years. The biblical account concludes, "Jacob lay with Rachel also, and he loved Rachel more than Leah. And he worked for Laban another seven years" (Gen. 29:30).

One wouldn't have to be a psychologist to predict the problems that were about to arise in that household. Can you imagine the conflicting emotions Laban's cruel deception produced? Jacob, the deceiver who had cheated his brother of their father's blessing, was outdone in deception by Laban! He ended up doing seven more years of hard labor without pay for a woman he didn't want in the first place. This was not exactly a great start for a marriage—especially one with two wives.

There was a physical difference between Leah and

Rachel. Leah was older, had weak or delicate eyes, and apparently was not attractive. Rachel was younger and had a beautiful face and figure. Scripture simply states the sad truth: "And Jacob loved Rachel more than Leah."

## An Unloved Wife

We can't blame Jacob. He'd made his choice almost from the moment he saw Rachel, and it's impossible to drum up romantic love on demand. Can you imagine how difficult it was for Leah to see Jacob's passionate love for Rachel, knowing that he didn't feel the same way about her at all? This was living in daily pain. She must have experienced both jealousy and envy. But God has a way of evening things out:

"When the LORD saw that Leah was not loved, he opened her womb, but Rachel was barren. Leah became pregnant and gave birth to a son. She named him Reuben, for she said, 'It is because the LORD has seen my misery. Surely my husband will love me now.' . . .

"When Rachel saw that she was not bearing Jacob any children, she became jealous of her sister. So she said to Jacob, 'Give me children, or I'll die!'

"Jacob became angry with her and said, 'Am I in the place of God, who has kept you from having children?'" (Gen. 29:31–32; 30:1–2).

Rachel had what Leah wanted—Jacob's love. But now she was jealous of Leah because she wanted what Leah had—children. In that day, it was a great reproach upon a woman if she did not give her husband sons. Jacob put the blame where it belonged, on God.

The rivalry between these two sisters increased as they tried to build their families with strategies that were normal for that culture. Sometimes a wife gave her maid to her husband sexually, and the maid became pregnant. When the child was born, the wife would catch the child on her knees and thus claim him as her own. Rachel did it first, then Leah followed suit. Both of them were in this battle to the bitter end. But the difference in the characters of the two women is revealed in Genesis 30:14–16: "During wheat harvest, Reuben went out into the fields and found some mandrake plants, which he brought to his mother Leah. Rachel said to Leah, 'Please give me some of your son's mandrakes.'

"But she said to her, 'Wasn't it enough that you took away my husband? Will you take my son's mandrakes too?'

"'Very well,' Rachel said, 'he can sleep with you tonight in return for your son's mandrakes.'"

## Forever Dissatisfied

Apparently, Rachel even used her power over Jacob to orchestrate his sex life and keep him from sleeping with Leah so she wouldn't have any more children! In essence, Leah had to "hire" Jacob from Rachel for a night. She did so in exchange for some mandrake roots that Rachel supposed would make her fertile. But God continued to give children only to Leah. She had six sons and one daughter of her own before Rachel had her first son.

"Then God remembered Rachel; he listened to her and opened her womb. She became pregnant and gave birth to a son and said, 'God has taken away my disgrace.' She named him Joseph, and said, 'May the LORD add to me another son'" (Gen. 30:22–24).

Nothing was ever enough for Rachel. Instead of thanking God for her one son, she had to have more. She had to catch up with her sister. That's a classic symptom of envy—it is insatiable.

## Rachel's Immature Spirit

We see further evidence of Rachel's lack of maturity when God told Jacob to go back to his homeland. He told his wives his plans, and Rachel and Leah replied, "Do we still have any share in the inheritance of our father's estate? Does he not regard us as foreigners? Not only has he sold us, but he has used up what was paid for us. Surely all the wealth that God took away from our father belongs to us and our children. So do whatever God has told you" (Gen. 31:14–16).

After thirteen years, the two women were still bitter toward their father for the way he had exploited them and the misery his actions had caused. But there was a difference in the spiritual quality of the two women. One particular thing Rachel did demonstrates, after twenty years of knowing and living with Jacob, that his faith in God had made little impact on her spiritual understanding. We know this because we're told, "When Laban had gone to shear his sheep, Rachel stole her father's household gods" (Gen. 31:19).

Laban was a man who worshiped many gods. The fact that Rachel stole them tells us several things about her. First of all, she still had pagan tendencies if she thought these little figurines would bring blessings. She also may have thought that they gave her a right to claim her father's inheritance. Whatever the reason, she deceived both her father and her husband. When Laban accused Jacob of stealing the idols, Jacob, in righteous indignation, unknowingly condemned his beloved wife to death. He raged, "But if you find anyone who has your gods, he shall not live" (Gen. 31:32).

Rachel was saved from discovery only because she hid the idols in her camel saddle and sat on it, then lied and claimed she couldn't get up because she was having her period. No one would search her saddle, because anything a woman sat on during her menses was made unclean.

Rachel was both a liar and a thief; she deceived her father and her husband. Rachel was lovely on the outside, but her character wasn't very beautiful. External beauty can be a hindrance to character development, and Rachel was envious, jealous, selfish, manipulative, greedy, and unsatisfied. Still, her husband's passion and preference for her lasted all her life.

Notice also how Jacob arranged his family in order of preference when he thought Esau still wanted revenge: "Jacob looked up and there was Esau, coming with his four hundred men; so he divided the children among Leah, Rachel and the two maidservants. He put the maidservants and their children in front, Leah and her children next, and Rachel and Joseph in the rear" (Gen 33:1–2).

How do you think Leah felt? No matter how many children she had, Jacob would never love her as much as he loved Rachel. Meanwhile, Rachel could have been gracious and generous to her unloved older sister, but she wasn't. We don't read of her doing a single kind, unselfish act. Finally she became pregnant with the second son she wanted, but this time it cost her her life to bear him: "And as she was having great difficulty in childbirth, the mid-wife said to her, 'Don't be afraid, for you have another son.' As she breathed her last—for she was dying—she named her son Ben-Oni. But his father named him Benjamin" (Gen. 35:17–18).

Jacob's favorite wife was buried by the wayside. Leah was eventually buried by Jacob's side in the cave at Machpelah with Abraham and Sarah, Isaac and Rebekah. What havoc jealousy and envy wrought upon this family!

Are those same destructive emotions doing a number

on you? In case you aren't aware of the symptoms of jealousy and envy, give yourself this test taken from material developed by Les Carter in his book *Mind Over Emotions*:[2]

- Do you work extremely hard to come out looking good?
- Do you examine others with a critical eye?
- Do you have hidden feelings of inferiority?
- Do you complain about not getting fair treatment?
- Do you have an insatiable desire for success?
- Do you need a lot of recognition for your achievements?
- Do you tend to be status conscious?
- Do you find it hard to pay compliments to others?
- Do you keep score of your own good deeds and those of others?
- Are you willing to pass along negative rumors about a successful person?
- Do you put on a false front in order to appear impressive?
- Do you base your self-image on your performance?

If you answered yes to some of these questions, you may be having trouble with envy, even though you haven't recognized it.

## Causes of Envy

Like many other emotions, envy is a symptom of other, underlying issues that need to be resolved. Les Carter includes these examples as sources of envy: being overly concerned with personal rights, taking other people's success personally, desiring selfish gain, yearning for status and achievement, and an inability to share.[3] Let's take a closer look at each of these sources.

## Being Overly Concerned with Personal Rights

We hear a lot about rights today. It appears that individual rights are increasing at the same time personal responsibility is decreasing. We are moving rapidly toward the idea that government is supposed to meet every need of the citizen and society is to blame for every crime.

Individuals blame their difficulties on their parents, their poverty, their lack of education, a past traumatic experience, or any number of other culprits. At the same time, they never seem to take the responsibility for their own actions.

Personal rights must be balanced with personal responsibility. There's a difference between the "right to life, liberty, and happiness" and the right to pursue life, liberty, and happiness. Pursuit involves effort on the part of the pursuer. Everyone does not have an inalienable right to wealth, a new car, and a college education. We are responsible to pursue these goals, but they are not rights.

## Taking Other People's Success Personally

Suppose someone you know is good at doing something, and it's something at which you aren't very gifted. When that happens, watch out. Envy can rear its ugly head, and you'll find yourself resenting every success the other person has.

I would love to be able to arrange flowers the way my friend Sarah Mitchell does. I've even tried to have her teach me. But I will never be able to arrange flowers with the creativity and ease she demonstrates. So I have a choice: I can resent Sarah's success when I compare it with my failure, or I can acknowledge her skill and be thankful that she will arrange flowers for me!

## Desiring Selfish Gain

Envy starts with desire. We all want things we don't have: money, a nice figure, a better home, or more clothes. We long for a happy marriage, successful children, a secure, pleasurable job. There's nothing wrong with these desires as long as we are realistic, recognizing that they do not bestow value on our lives.

However, if and when these things become essential to us, we will look with the green eyes of envy at everyone who has what we want. We'll keep working harder and more desperately to reach our goals without ever being content. Eventually, we will be under the full-time control of envy, a brutal taskmaster. We should never forget what John D. Rockefeller said when he was asked how much money is enough. "Just one more dollar," was his sage reply.

## Yearning for Status and Achievement

There's nothing wrong with wanting recognition for our achievements. But at times that craving can become a competitive spirit that has to outdo everyone else. When that happens, you can be sure envy is at the root.

Today's society values people for their appearance or their achievements. It is very difficult not to be envious of the woman with a beautiful figure when you struggle daily to not gain a pound. It's hard to feel good about ourselves when we've been driving the same car for ten years while others are enjoying this year's luxury models. We don't accept ourselves as we are; we are unable to recognize our own strengths. Instead, we compare our weaknesses with others' strengths, and consequently we feel envious.

## An Inability to Share

It's difficult for the envious person to share in the joys of other people, especially when someone else is getting what the envious one wants and doesn't have. I admire women who are struggling with infertility when I see them attending baby showers for others and sharing their joy. They may go home and weep afterward, but they are genuinely happy for their friends.

## Overcoming Jealousy and Envy

Perhaps as you've read this chapter, you've seen indications that jealousy or envy is an unwelcome aspect of your character. Of course it is God's will for you to overcome that negative emotion, and there are some concrete steps you can take to do so.

### Recognize That You Are Envious or Jealous

Acknowledging your envy means looking at yourself honestly. Galatians 5:19–21 tells us that envy is a product of our sinful human nature. Ask the Holy Spirit to reveal to you whether your ulterior motives are for selfish gain or to achieve status in other people's eyes. Name envy for what it is. Blow away the cover-up.

### Choose with Your Will to Get Rid of It

Harboring envy keeps us from hungering for God's Word, and God's Word is vital for us to continue to grow spiritually. "Therefore, rid yourselves of all malice and all deceit, hypocrisy, envy and slander of every kind. Like newborn babies, crave pure spiritual milk, so that by it you may grow up in your salvation, now that you have tasted that the Lord is good" (1 Pet. 2:1–2).

Galatians 5:26 says envy will also keep us from living the Spirit-controlled life God wants for His children. It's a deadly deterrent to spiritual growth. By making a choice of the will then asking God to empower us, we can decide to overcome envy or jealousy. With His help, we will do so.

## Confess It As Sin and Accept Forgiveness

We've already learned the value of 1 John 1:9. God promises to forgive and cleanse us from all sin if we agree with Him that what we are doing is sin. Once we've accepted His forgiveness, we are able to start on a new path.

## Accept Yourself As You Are with Gratitude

Develop a thankful heart. Thank God every day that you are just the person He created you to be. Thank Him that He chose you to be His own. Thank Him for your face and figure, your health, your abilities, your family, your job, your bank account, your friends. Thank Him for the spiritual gifts that make you necessary to the body of believers. Make sure, while you're thanking Him, that you don't compare yourself with others.

## Learn the Joy of Giving to Others

Envy is rooted in selfishness. It's only concerned with satisfying the cravings of the envious person. There's a way to show that we are changing on the inside. When we share our material possessions, praise the success of others, and encourage others in reaching their goals, we will begin to experience the joy that comes from giving. By doing the opposite of our sinful nature, we change our habit patterns and demonstrate to God that we are working with Him in renewing our minds.

## Keep Earthly Achievements in Eternal Perspective

When our lives are over, we're going to leave everything behind. The body we spend so much money on will return to dust. The wardrobe, the beautiful home, the bank account, the advanced degree, the recognition—all those things that we give our lives to are going to remain on Planet Earth long after we've departed.

There are no pockets in a shroud. That's why it's essential to remember that only two things on earth will enter eternity—people and God's Word. If we give priority to giving God's word to people and living it, we'll have something that will last forever.

## Set Your Heart on Heavenly Things

When we trusted Jesus Christ, we received a new nature. And we became citizens of a new homeland—heaven. "Since, then, you have been raised with Christ, set your hearts on things above, where Christ is seated at the right hand of God. Set your minds on things above, not on earthly things" (Col. 3:1–2).

It's God's intention that our hearts and minds ought to be focused on new goals, and that our conduct should be controlled by new standards. As we deliberately turn away from the old and embrace the new, we are not going to keep looking over our shoulder to see who's catching up with us. Instead, we'll follow the Spirit's leading for our own lives and choose to be grateful for everything God does for us. This will ultimately be the way envy is routed out of our hearts.

Once it is removed, we will begin to experience joy and contentment and the sense of personal significance that Jesus brings will blossom beautifully and fragrantly in our lives.

# 10

## The Reality
## of Rejection

KATHY, AN ASPIRING YOUNG WRITER, received a telephone call from a local pastor. "You did such a great job of editing my sermon transcripts into booklets, I suggested to Martha Frazier that you do the same for her. Do you know who she is?"

Kathy frowned, trying to place the name. The pastor continued, "Martha has a unique ministry, teaching Bible classes on the North Side. She's a bit eccentric," he chuckled briefly, "but she's got some great things to say. I recommended you highly, and she wants you to attend her Bible study tomorrow afternoon. She'll meet with you afterward. Oh, and she said she'd leave your name at the gate."

"What gate?"

"The study is probably in a gated community."

Delighted with the job referral, Kathy checked her map after hanging up. Martha's meeting was on the North Side, all right. It was in the most affluent section of the city, where the properties started at 1.5 million dollars and went up from there. Kathy's next stop was her closet. What on earth would she wear? She and Bill managed to pay the rent, to make the car payments, and to eat. There wasn't much left for clothes—especially the kind she needed for a job interview on Martha's side of town.

"Oh well," she told herself, "I'll wear a skirt and sweater. Nothing wrong with that . . ."

The next day, as Kathy dressed carefully, she was frustrated to find that she had a run in every pair of pantyhose she owned. She shrugged off the inconvenience, jumped in her not-so-clean Suzuki, and headed for the Bible study a few minutes early. After passing through two ornate steel gates and parking directly in front of an enormous mansion, she found her way to the front door.

The hostess eyed her coolly, then glanced at the street. "Is that your, uh, Jeep, dear?"

"Yes, it's mine. Didn't have time to wash it . . ." she laughed apologetically.

"Would you mind terribly moving it around the corner? We're expecting some special guests. Thank you so much, dear."

Glancing at the woman's huge diamond ring, bejeweled cross, and three diamond bracelets, Kathy was acutely aware of the run in her nylons. She realized her inexpensive clothes looked unmatched and tacky as she meekly reparked the car, and her hair kept sticking to the sweat on her forehead. Walking back toward the large house, she noticed two black Mercedes Benz sedans pulling up in front. The women who got out were impeccably dressed, perfectly manicured, and evidently knew each other very well—so well, in fact, that they failed to speak to Kathy.

Kathy found a seat in the back of the room, which was beautifully arranged with several rows of chairs and a table of hors d'oeuvres. She decided against taking anything to eat—by now her stomach was in knots, and she didn't want anyone to notice her. No one did.

After the Bible lesson, which was dramatically presented by Martha Frazier, Kathy waited at the front to speak to her. When she explained to Ms. Frazier her reason for attending, she noticed the older woman's eyes scanning her, head to toe. Was Martha Frazier naturally unfriendly, or did she simply dislike Kathy? How could she? They'd never met before. There was an uncomfortable feeling about their brief conversation, after which Kathy handed the teacher her business card and all but ran toward her car.

"We'll be in touch," Ms. Frazier had said as they parted.

Two days later, Kathy received a note from Martha Frazier, perfectly typed on her elegant letterhead. "Unfortunately, I don't feel you are the right person to edit my lessons into booklets. You clearly are not familiar with the type of woman to whom God has given me the privilege of ministering. Thank you, however, for attending the study. I trust you were blessed."

Kathy's eyes blurred with tears of shame and humiliation as she read the note. She knew very well why she had been rejected for the job—she didn't look like the other women there. They were rich. She wasn't. They were sophisticated. She was not. "She's right . . ." she said aloud as she ripped the note in half and angrily threw it in the trash. "Not only am I unfamiliar with that type of woman, I can't imagine how they can possibly call themselves Christians!"

# The Reality of Rejection

## Rejection—An All-Too-Familiar Experience

To reject someone means to refuse to grant that person recognition or acceptance, to discard that individual as being worthless. Have you ever felt rejected?

- Did you feel rejected because your father was distant and cold, too busy to give you time and attention?

- Did you feel rejected because your mother favored your older sister who was prettier or smarter?

- Did you feel rejected because you weren't gifted in athletics and when the class divided up into teams, you were the last one chosen?

- Did you feel rejected because your school clothes were not as nice as the other kids' and they made fun of you?

- Were you fat? Were you plain looking? Did you have acne? Did you have to wear thick glasses?

- Were you rejected during your high school years because you weren't popular; did you miss your prom because no one invited you?

- Were you rejected for membership in a sorority you wanted to join in college?

- Were you passed over for promotion at work because someone else was younger or prettier?

- Did you lose your job because you were getting older?

- Did you date a man for several years, expecting to marry him, only to have him back out?

- Do you feel rejected by your children, after giving your life to raise them and to provide for them the benefits you didn't have?

- Did your husband leave you in midlife for another woman—or worse yet, another man?

Rejection is a painful experience no matter what the cause, and all too often, we don't assign enough blame to the rejecter. We simply agree with his or her evaluation of us and carry a feeling of inferiority or of being "damaged goods" all our lives.

## Rejection Is Not a Measure of True Worth

But does rejection really affect our basic worth? If individuals don't appreciate me as a total person because they don't like my looks or my performance, does that mean I really am what they think I am? Am I intrinsically less valuable? Should I permit them to label me for the rest of my life? What if they are wrong?

They usually are.

As we considered Jacob's two wives, Leah and Rachel, in the last chapter, we learned how envy and jealousy can destroy harmony and love in a family. As we study the emotional obstacle of rejection, let's take a closer look at Leah's spiritual journey, because Leah was a woman who lived with the pain of rejection every day of her life.

First of all, Leah was never respected by her father. In that day, it was the father's responsibility to arrange for his daughters to marry. During the seven years Jacob worked for Rachel, Laban could have tried to find a husband for Leah. If he had offered a big-enough dowry, he would have found someone to marry her. But apparently he thought she was hopeless as a marriage prospect and the only way to get rid of her was to palm her off on poor Jacob, who was besotted with love for Rachel. Laban passed Leah off to Jacob like a dishonest businessman getting rid of damaged goods at full price.

## Leah: Unwanted, Unloved

Can you imagine how Leah must have cringed when Jacob looked at her in the morning light with shock, distaste, and anger? That terrible deception on Jacob's wedding night set in motion much of the grief that family experienced for decades to come. Sadly, Leah didn't deserve that rejection. Apparently, her rejection was based on her looks—her weak eyes. Nobody noticed her character, her inner self, or her mind. This isn't much different than the way things are today. You've never seen an ugly Miss America, have you?

"Jacob loved Rachel more than Leah." If we think at all about those six little words from Genesis 29:30, we will be able to imagine the many ways Jacob demonstrated his feelings. But we also see how God expressed His feelings for Leah. As we learned in the last chapter, God stepped in to let Leah know she was valuable to Him by allowing her to bear children. Still, Leah suffered her husband's rejection, so from her we can learn some important principles for handling rejection.

## Face the Facts Realistically

Leah knew she wasn't loved. She wasn't fooled, and she didn't fool herself. Sometimes we make excuses and cover up for the people who reject us, because if we acknowledge their cruelty, it hurts too much. Worse yet, we keep on trying to be accepted and as a result face rejection over and over.

Leah's longing for Jacob's love probably lasted all her life, but she learned to live with the situation. Her spiritual journey led her to reality and acceptance, and her awareness of God indicates a stable relationship with Him that sustained her and gave her the strength to endure her painful circumstances. Her spiritual growth is reflected in the names she gave her children:

"Leah became pregnant and gave birth to a son. She named him Reuben, for she said, 'It is because the LORD has seen my misery. Surely my husband will love me now'" (Gen. 29:32).

Reuben means, "See, a son" but when it is pronounced in Hebrew, it sounds like "He has seen my misery." What does that tell us about Leah's life? She was miserable! Listen to her heart's cry: "Surely my husband will love me now." We learn something important from her.

## Don't Pretend; Confess Your Feelings

To accept the way things are and to admit you would like them to be different are two different matters. It isn't "spiritual" to pretend that everything's fine and you aren't really hurt when you are. Tell the Lord how you feel. He knows it anyway. And, if you can, share your feelings with a trustworthy friend who will pray for you. Both of these honest expressions are important to your emotional and spiritual health.

Despite the birth of Reuben, Leah remained unloved. As the account continues, "She conceived again, and when she gave birth to a son she said, 'Because the LORD heard that I am not loved, he gave me this one too.' So she named him Simeon" (Gen. 29:33).

Simeon means, "One who hears." Leah believed that because the Lord had heard that she was not loved, He had given her another son as a consolation prize. What exactly *did* God hear? Was Leah told in words that she was unloved? By whom? Did Rachel spitefully remind Leah that she was the booby prize as Rachel's jealousy increased because she was barren? Or did this mean that Leah told God in her prayers about her rejection? Sadly, both scenarios were probably true.

Before long, Leah had another son: "Again she conceived, and when she gave birth to a son she said, 'Now at last my husband will become attached to me, because I have borne him three sons.' So he was named Levi" (Gen. 29:34).

Levi sounds like the word "attached" in Hebrew. This time Leah lowered her expectations. Now she would be satisfied with just some feeling of genuine connection from Jacob and some appreciation. She never mentions love again. It seems she had finally faced the fact that Jacob would probably never love her as he did Rachel.

## Give Up Unrealistic Expectations

Sometimes we make ourselves unhappy by envisioning changes that aren't going to take place. Your mother may never be a warm, loving person. Your father may never tell you verbally that he loves you. Your husband may never be able to let down the walls of protection he has built around himself and share the intimacy you long for.

If you spend your life focused on making some other person change, you're wasting your energy. The problem is not yours; the fault does not lie with you. You are not unworthy. Instead, the other person may be incapable of the normal responses of an emotionally healthy person.

We see this happen in Leah when a very important shift occurs in her focus after her fourth son is born: "She conceived again, and when she gave birth to a son she said, 'This time I will praise the LORD.' So she named him Judah. Then she stopped having children" (Gen. 29:35).

Judah means "praise." After years of pain, Leah's entire focus turned to God. This time she didn't mention Jacob at all; instead she got her sense of worth from God. She knew God valued her because He had proved it to her in a way that was understood in that culture. He gave her children. She was devalued by her father. She was rejected by her husband. She was envied by her sister. But she was loved by God, and that fact gave her the strength to go on.

## Shift your Focus to God's Acceptance of You

Take a moment, open your Bible, and read Ephesians 1:3–14. Look how special we are to God! We are:

Blessed
> Chosen
>> Loved
>>> Predestined
>>>> Adopted
>>>>> Redeemed
>>>>>> Forgiven
>>>>>>> Lavished with grace
>>>>>>>> Included in Christ
>>>>>>>>> Sealed with the Spirit
>>>>>>>>>> Guaranteed an inheritance

When we trust Christ and establish a relationship with Him, He accepts us with arms wide open. His acceptance is what gives us value. It is from Him that we should derive our self-image.

Don't give the person or persons who reject you permission to put a price tag on you. God has put *His* price tag on you. You are worth so much to Him that He came Himself to die for you so you could be His son or daughter, born into His family by faith in Jesus Christ. Follow Leah's example!

## Praise the Lord!

Soon after that, Leah stopped bearing children, and she followed Rachel's lead in giving her maid to Jacob so she could have more sons. Even the names Leah gave those sons born to her maid indicated a thankful attitude: "Good fortune" and "Happy."

## Be Thankful for God's Gifts

Focusing on God doesn't mean we won't ever feel resentment at unfair treatment. Leah wasn't perfect, either. When Rachel tried to prevent her from having more children by keeping Jacob from sleeping with her, she demeaned herself by "hiring" him for the night with her son's mandrakes. But she also must have prayed, because we read, "God listened to Leah, and she became pregnant and bore Jacob a fifth son. Then Leah said, 'God has rewarded me for giving my maidservants to my husband.' So she named him Issachar" (Gen. 30:17–18).

I don't think God gave Leah another son because she gave her maid to Jacob. I believe He answered her prayer simply because He loved her. Even today, we often have wrong concepts about God, although we possess the complete revelation of Scripture. And remember, Leah had no

Bible. Everything Leah knew about God had been transmitted orally, mostly from Jacob, and Jacob clearly didn't understand the grace of God.

And even then God wasn't through showering Leah with His blessings: "Then Leah said, 'God has presented me with a precious gift. This time my husband will treat me with honor, because I have borne him six sons.' So she named him Zebulun" (Gen. 30:20–21).

Another son, and she welcomed him as a precious gift from God. Now she was willing to settle for even less—she just wanted her husband to give her the honor due her as the mother of his six sons. As a special blessing, we read that she also gave birth to a daughter, and she named her Dinah.

How easy it is to overlook God's blessings because there is something we *don't* have. Sometimes our "if onlys" blind us to the wonderful provisions we have received, and we refuse to be wholeheartedly grateful.

## Life Can Be Unfair

We will all experience pain in this world if we live long enough. This is a fallen world, and we are a fallen race. There's no way to escape suffering. Instead, if we accept it and trust God to use it, He will work it out for our good. God has a way of compensating us for our hurts. And as we learn to deal with adversity, our personal character develops.

Leah was the mother of half of Jacob's sons, and half of the twelve tribes of Israel descended from her. Yet she lived with rejection all her life—her father's, her husband's, and her sister's. But God proved His acceptance of her in a language she could understand by giving her six sons and a daughter.

Jacob chose Rachel. God chose Leah.

Rachel had what Leah longed for, but it didn't make her a better person. We see no evidence of contentment or gratitude in Rachel's life. And there is no reason to believe that she had a relationship with the Lord comparable to Leah's. Apparently, the pain of rejection caused Leah to turn to the Lord, and in doing so, she found her contentment in Him.

In the long term, God had the greatest blessing of all in store for Leah, even though she didn't live to see it. God chose Judah, Leah's son, to be the father of the royal dynasty through which His Messiah would be born: Christ, the Son of David, Lion of the tribe of Judah. And, like His grandmother generations before Him, Jesus was rejected too.

## Our Savior Experienced Total Rejection

"He was despised and rejected by men, a man of sorrows, and familiar with suffering. . . . And we esteemed him not" (Isa. 53:3).

Jesus was perfect. There was no sin, no personality or character flaw in Him that caused Him to be rejected. Yet He suffered undeserved rejection all His life. Jesus was rejected by His peers, by His half-brothers, by His nation, by the Gentiles, by the world He had created. In the hour of His agony He was betrayed by one friend, denied by another, and abandoned by all of His disciples. He experienced loneliness, suffering, grief, and rejection. "Surely he took up our infirmities and carried our sorrows, yet we considered him stricken by God, smitten by him and afflicted" (Isa. 53:4).

Why did Jesus endure such agony? He bore our sins on the cross and took our punishment so that *we* might be forgiven. But in so doing He endured a rejection we will never know. He even felt rejected by God, His Father. Remember His cry from the cross, "My God! My God! Why have you forsaken me?" (Matt. 27:46).

When Jesus became man, He bore the full penalty for our sin, which is separation from God: "By his wounds we are healed" (Isa. 53:5).

In the New Testament, we learn more about Jesus' rejection: "He came to that which was his own, but his own did not receive him. Yet to all who received him, to those who believed in his name, he gave the right to become children of God" (John 1:11–12).

When you trust Christ as your Savior, you are born into God's family. God accepts you as His beloved child. He loves you with a love that will never waver, falter, or end. And as you grow in your new life, your great High Priest Jesus intercedes for you with God. Here's the kind of priest He is:

"For we do not have a high priest who is unable to sympathize with our weaknesses, but we have one who has been tempted in every way, just as we are—yet without sin. Let us then approach the throne of grace with confidence, so that we may receive mercy and find grace to help us in our time of need" (Heb. 4:15–16).

## Jesus Is a Compassionate, Sympathetic Intercessor

Jesus knows how rejection makes us feel. He has been there. He will comfort us, give us value, and use our pain to help others. But to appropriate these gifts, we have to make the kinds of decisions Leah did. We have to give up our expectations and focus on God, praising and thanking Him for who He is and for the blessings He showers on us. If we do that, rejection will not be a hindrance to our spiritual growth. It will become a catalyst.

George Matheson was a brilliant young man who was engaged to a woman he loved very much. Like Leah, he was troubled by weak eyes and was told that he would soon be totally blind. Just before their wedding, his fiancée told him she wouldn't marry him because she couldn't face life with a blind man. Matheson never married. But the wounds of this rejection gave us a hymn that has comforted countless thousands of God's children. The words trace for us the journey we must all take:

*O Love that wilt not let me go.*
*I rest my weary soul in thee;*
*I give thee back the life I owe,*
*That in thine ocean depths its flow*
*May richer, fuller be.*

*O Light that followest all my way,*
*I yield my flick'ring torch to thee;*
*My heart restores its borrowed ray*
*That in thy sunshine's blaze its day*
*May brighter, fairer be.*

*O Joy that seekest me through pain*
*I cannot close my heart to thee.*
*I trace the rainbow through the rain*
*And feel the promise is not vain*
*That morn shall tearless be.*

*O Cross that liftest up my head*
*I dare not ask to fly from thee;*
*I lay in dust, life's glory dead,*
*And from the ground there blossoms red*
*Life that shall endless be.*

# 11

## Greed: A Fearful Master

LYNNE BLAKE WAS A SUCCESSFUL FEMALE executive who had been very fortunate in the real estate business. By the time she was thirty-five years old, she was ready to open her own office. And she was determined to make it the most high-tech, state-of-the-art real estate office in town.

Three weeks before the "Lynne Blake Real Estate" sign lit up and the office officially opened, Lynne ordered four expensive computers complete with printers, modems, CD-ROMs, and sound cards. "Why do we need four computers?" her assistant Brenda asked. "There are only two of us."

"We'll be expanding soon," Lynne smiled. "And until we do, I want people to know we're on the cutting edge of this business!"

The next day, four top-of-the-line office chairs were delivered. An account executive from a voice mail system signed Lynne up for his most complete setup. In the days to come, a stream of deliveries brought gourmet coffee service, customized paper stock, exotic plants, and every other imaginable office accessory.

Meanwhile, Lynne was dressing in the finest executive wardrobe she could assemble. She never showed up at work wearing less than five hundred dollars' worth of clothing. "It's part of the package," she winked at Brenda after she had complimented her on yet another new suit.

Lynne's parents were extremely wealthy and had agreed to underwrite her new business, so the sky was the limit as far as finances were concerned. Once Lynne and Brenda settled into a routine, rather than hire two new employees, Lynne simply doubled Brenda's workload. This, of course, saved her another salary.

Exactly one year after the new business opened its doors under Lynne's ownership, to Brenda's horror all the computers were removed—donated to a local charity. In their place, four newer, faster models were installed, promising more speed, memory, and complicated software.

Brenda rushed into Lynne's office, visibly upset. "Lynne, I'm just learning this system, and now I have to learn a whole new one! We don't need more memory or more speed on our computers. We just need another person to help input the information!"

Lynne was annoyed with Brenda's objection. "It's none of your business, Brenda. You have nothing to complain about."

"Well, if you aren't going to hire someone else, it wouldn't hurt you to invest a little money in me—why don't you give me a raise? Why are you spending every dime on stuff we don't even need when I'm breaking my neck for you?"

Lynne snapped, "I'll spend my money any way I want! This equipment makes your work a piece of cake. Why should I give you a raise? You're lucky to have a job at all. You can quit if you're unhappy."

## Would You Call Yourself a Materialistic Person?

Most of us aren't hooked on equipping suburban real estate offices with high-tech equipment. But we all face the temptation to spend more than we should on things we don't really need. For example . . .

- How many catalogs have you received in the mail recently?

- How many things in those catalogs would you like to have?

- How many items do you usually buy when you're "window shopping" at the mall?

- Do you need what you buy, or do you simply want it?

- Do you have more "stuff" than you have space in which to store it?

- Does buying new clothes make you feel better? For how long?

- Do you use cash or a credit card? Are your credit cards maxed out?

Will we ever be satisfied with what we have? The answer is *no* if we are gripped in the vise of greed and its twin sister, materialism. To be materialistic is to take interest exclusively, chiefly, or excessively in the material or bodily necessities and comforts of life. To be greedy is to never have enough.

Is it possible to be a believer and a materialist at the same time? Yes, most definitely. But it's *not* possible to be a committed, growing believer with divided priorities: Money is God's great rival for our hearts. Jesus said, "No man can serve two masters. Either he will hate the one and love the other or he will be devoted to the one and despise the other. You cannot serve both God and Money" (Luke 16:13).

The love of money and the things it can buy makes us greedy for more, no matter how much we have. As Scripture teaches us, "Whoever loves money never has money enough; whoever loves wealth is never satisfied with his income" (Eccles. 5:10).

Have you noticed that we're talking about a love affair with money? Love of money will impede our growth to maturity because it keeps us from loving God with all our heart, soul, mind, and strength. Greed results in displacing the One who has the right to be King on the throne of our lives. That's why greed is called "idolatry" in Colossians 3:5.

## A King Who Wanted More

We have a perfect example of what greed can lead to in Ahab, king of Israel. Ahab had just about everything but character, and he was married to a woman who was even worse than he was, Jezebel. He was very wealthy. He had one entire palace inlaid with ivory. And he had another palace in Jezreel. One day as he looked out the window of his Jezreel palace he saw a vineyard that he thought would make a nice vegetable garden for himself. The only problem was it belonged to someone else, a man named Naboth. Here's what happened:

"Ahab said to Naboth, 'Let me have your vineyard to use for a vegetable garden, since it is close to my palace. In exchange I will give you a better vineyard or, if you prefer, I will pay you whatever it is worth'" (1 Kings 21:2–3).

Naboth refused to sell because he was obedient to God's instructions about the land. When Israel first took possession of the land, every family received their plot of ground. The land could never be permanently sold and was to remain in that family's possession forever. But instead of respecting Naboth's reasons for not selling, look what Ahab did:

"Ahab went home, sullen and angry because Naboth the Jezreelite had said, 'I will not give you the inheritance of my fathers.' He lay on his bed sulking and refused to eat" (1 Kings 21:4).

Real mature, wasn't he? But he demonstrates something we all do. He focused on what he didn't have. Ahab expressed no gratitude for all his wealth, his power, or his palaces. Instead, he lay on his bed sulking and fasting in protest for not getting his way.

How do you react when you don't get what you want? Maybe you want to redecorate the bedroom, order new carpet or furniture, but your husband isn't ready for that. Maybe he's saying no because you're over the limit on all your credit cards. Or it may be that he just doesn't agree with you about the need for such things. Maybe he's tight with money. Whatever the reason, *your* reaction is your responsibility.

Do you shop around and find the best prices and show him how much you'll save by doing some things yourself? Do you pray and tell the Lord you are willing to wait for His timing? Or do you nag, sulk, and give your husband the silent treatment? Ahab sulked and fasted long enough to irritate Jezebel, who is a perfect example of what a wife *shouldn't* be. When she found out about Naboth's refusal to give up his vineyard, she came up with a plot to get Naboth murdered. And because she was queen, her plan worked perfectly.

"When Ahab heard that Naboth was dead, he got up and went down to take possession of Naboth's vineyard" (1 Kings 21:16).

Rampant greed led to the murder of an innocent man and the confiscation of his property. But God had seen it all. Elijah the prophet met Ahab when he went to take possession of Naboth's vineyard, and he pronounced God's punishment upon Ahab for what he and Jezebel had done. His grim prophecy predicted that dogs would lick up the couple's blood and that God would wipe out their descendants from the face of the earth—the worst imaginable curse for an Israelite. God already had a great deal against Ahab and Jezebel, but their greed-inspired brutality against Naboth was the last straw.

## Greed—God's Rival for Our Hearts

Greed is diametrically opposed to all that Scripture has to say about the place money and things should have in our lives. One out of every seven verses in the book of Luke is on the subject of money. In Luke 12, Jesus was approached by a man who wanted more of his inheritance than he was entitled to. In that culture, the older brother received twice what the other brothers received because of the responsibilities involved in being the head of the family. Instead of arbitrating this man's grievance, Jesus addressed the heart of the issue.

"Someone in the crowd said to him, 'Teacher, tell my brother to divide the inheritance with me.'

"Jesus replied, 'Man, who appointed me a judge or an arbiter between you?' Then he said to them, 'Watch out! Be on your guard against all kinds of greed; a man's life does not consist in the abundance of his possessions'" (Luke 12:13–15).

How do you measure the quality of your life? What makes it valuable? Perhaps you think in terms of what you have accomplished—your education, your job, your home, your summer house, your clothes, your portfolio, your cars, your art. Jesus said that our lives do not consist of the abundance of our possessions. Real life is the life of the mind and the spirit. Real life is freedom from the greed that enslaves us, a freedom that reveals a right relationship with our Maker.

Next Jesus told a parable about a greedy man: "The ground of a certain rich man produced a good crop. He thought to himself, 'What shall I do? I have no place to store my crops.'

"Then he said, 'This is what I'll do. I will tear down my barns and build bigger ones, and there I will store all my grain and my goods. And I'll say to myself, 'You have plenty of good things laid up for many years. Take life easy; eat, drink and be merry.'

"But God said to him, 'You fool! This very night your life will be demanded from you. Then who will get what you have prepared for yourself?'" (Luke 12:16–21).

What could this man have done with all the wealth God had allowed him to accumulate? He could have used it unselfishly to help those in need. Instead, he decided that he would indulge himself in a hedonistic lifestyle. Unfortunately for him, that life was only one day long. God called him a fool because he was rich only in material things, and he used them for totally selfish pursuits—things that excluded God. He was rich, but not rich toward God.

How does one become rich toward God? Jesus explained to His disciples what that means: "Therefore I tell you, do not worry about your life, what you will eat; or about your body, what you will wear. Life is more than food, and the body more than clothes" (Luke 12:22–23).

## Principles for Greed-Free Living

To say we don't need to worry about how we will feed, clothe, and shelter ourselves doesn't mean we don't have to work to earn a living. It means we have a good reason not to be filled with anxiety about it. We have a Father in heaven who knows all about our needs. And, as we learned already, instead of worrying, our heavenly Father wants us to trust Him to supply these basic needs. God clothes and feeds birds and flowers, and we are much more valuable to Him than they are. God is the Creator of all things, but He is the heavenly Father of His children. And He is a good, wise, and loving Father. Here are some principles He offers to help us overcome our love of money and the things money buys.

### Make It Your Goal to Please God

One day Jesus Christ will be the ruler over the whole earth. But for now He must be the ruler on the throne of our hearts. He does not want us to be ruled by ourselves or our idols, whatever they may be. He said, "Seek his kingdom, and these things will be given to you as well" (Luke 12:31). A kingdom is a place where a king is sovereign. We seek God's kingdom when we live in obedience to Him and are involved in His interests.

If the Lord Jesus Christ is on our heart's throne, then we will accept the things He gives us as gifts from His hand. We will be grateful for whatever He chooses to give us. Jesus wants us to believe—and to live as if we believed—that the life of the spirit is more important than the life of the body. He told His disciples—and us: "Do not be afraid, little flock, for your Father has been pleased to give you the kingdom. Sell your possessions and give to the poor. Provide purses for yourselves that will not wear out, a treasure in heaven that will not be exhausted, where no thief comes near and no moth destroys. For where your treasure is, there your heart will be also" (Luke 12:32–34).

## Use Money to Build a Treasure in Heaven

The accumulation of money to be spent on things and pleasure should not be our goal. Scripture tells us, "Do not wear yourself out to get rich; have the wisdom to show restraint. Cast but a glance at riches, and they are gone, for they will surely sprout wings and fly off to the sky like an eagle" (Prov. 23:4–5). The contrast here is between the pursuit of earthly riches that can be lost and a heavenly treasure that is secure for eternity.

God gives us money to share with those who don't have it. He allows us to give so others will hear the gospel message and support the work of God's kingdom.

Where is your treasure? In a bank vault or in heaven? Do you give God His portion of your income? When we give to the Lord, we acknowledge that He is the Giver and Owner of all that we have and that we are only stewards of our possessions. God holds us responsible for the way we spend the money He supplies. Giving back to the Lord is also a way of saying thank you to Him for His love and care.

It demonstrates where our hearts are. These are ways of being rich toward God.

## Contentment Is a Cure for Greed

Are you content? Or is there always a gnawing dissatisfaction with something about your life? We come naked into the world, and we leave it naked. That puts money and possessions in proper perspective, doesn't it?

Consider Paul's advice to Timothy: "Godliness with contentment is great gain. For we brought nothing into the world, and we can take nothing out of it. But if we have food and clothing, we will be content with that. People who want to get rich fall into temptation and a trap and into many foolish and harmful desires that plunge men into ruin and destruction" (1 Tim. 6:6–9).

The desire for money and possessions leads to all kinds of sin. Men and women sacrifice their morality on the altar of greed. Husbands and wives neglect their families for the sake of a double income, a fact that has contributed to today's tragic disintegration of the family.

For the love of power and money, people compromise their ethical standards. There have been countless scandals in which men and women in public office have prostituted their positions for money. And church leaders haven't been far behind, making money their goal and fleecing the gullible to get it. This has caused the name of Christ to be blasphemed. The apostle Paul would not be surprised at such modern tragedies. As he wrote nearly two thousand years ago, "The love of money is a root of all kinds of evil. Some people, eager for money, have wandered from the faith and pierced themselves with many griefs" (1 Tim. 6:10).

## Love of Money Leads to Faithlessness and Sorrow

Notice God's Word doesn't say that money itself causes problems but rather it's the "love of money" that gets us into trouble. That's been the emphasis in all the passages we've studied. Money is neutral. However, when we make it our goal in life, it becomes the root of all kinds of evil.

Why does the love of money shipwreck our faith? Because the more secure we are financially, the less we depend on God to provide for us. We become independent; we think we don't need God. Instead of seeing God as the source of His bountiful provision and thanking Him, we take the credit for ourselves and fall into the trap of wanting more and more.

And many times when greed sets in, we are willing to bend all the rules to get more. We begin to look down on people who are not as successful as we are, so love and compassion for others is only a memory. A person can meet all kinds of grief on the road to riches.

The love of money has caused many mothers to hand their precious children over to paid workers to rear, not because they have to work, but because they choose to. They work either because they find their identity in a career rather than mothering, or because they want more things that money can buy and they won't discipline themselves to live within the means of one salary.

Of course I'm not referring to single mothers or to women who have to work because of financial adversity. But the grief that often comes through the neglect of children can't be consoled by a bank balance. For the believer, broken relationships, disappointments, and sorrows are self-inflicted wounds. They are the consequences of dethroning the Lord and enthroning money. That's why the apostle Paul again advised, "Command those who are rich in this present world not to be arrogant nor to put their hope in wealth, which is so uncertain, but to put their hope in God, who richly provides us with everything for our enjoyment" (1 Tim. 6:17).

## God Gives Us Material Blessings to Enjoy

God isn't concerned about our possessions. It's our attitude He cares about. Are we arrogant because we think we are better than someone who is poorer? Do we put our hope in wealth that can be lost, or on God who is eternal? Do we enjoy our possessions as gifts from a loving heavenly Father?

Do you enjoy your home, your china and silver, your window treatments, your furniture, your interior decorating, your patio, your yard, your clothes, and your car? Or do you look on them with a jaundiced eye, especially if you've just come from visiting someone with a much nicer home, wardrobe, or vehicle? When we keep the right perspective, God can trust us with more if He wants to. If we don't have the right perspective, we need to make a few attitude adjustments.

## Change Your Perspective and Pursuits

God's Word exhorts us to run as fast as we can from the goal of acquiring material possessions. Recognize it, confess it as sin, and pursue instead righteousness, godliness, faith, love, endurance, and gentleness: "But you, man of God, flee from all this, and pursue righteousness, godliness, faith, love, endurance and gentleness. Fight the good fight of the faith. Take hold of the eternal life to which you were called when you made your good confession in the presence of many witnesses" (1 Tim. 6:11–12).

Instead of grasping this temporal life, take a firm grasp on the eternal life we received when we trusted Jesus Christ as Lord and Savior. If we look at our short lives on earth through the grid of eternity, everything will be in focus and we will have the right priorities and accumulate treasures in heaven. We will follow Scripture's directive "to do good, to be rich in good deeds, and to be generous and willing to share. In this way they will lay up treasure for themselves as a firm foundation for the coming age, so that they may take hold of the life that is truly life" (1 Tim. 6:18–19).

## Give It Away Here to Store It in Heaven

Instead of defining our worth by our bank accounts, God wants us to be rich in good deeds, to be generous with our money, and to share with those who need it. "He who is kind to the poor lends to the LORD, and he will reward him for what he has done" (Prov. 19:17). God gives us money to use in His name, to do His work on earth. And God keeps very good records. He will reward us in His way—if not in our time here on earth, then definitely in eternity.

"Remember this: Whoever sows sparingly will also reap sparingly, and whoever sows generously will also reap generously. Each man should give what he has decided in his heart to give, not reluctantly or under compulsion, for God loves a cheerful giver. And God is able to make all grace abound to you, so that in all things at all times, having all that you need, you will abound in every good work. . . . You will be made rich in every way so that you can be generous on every occasion, and through us your generosity will result in thanksgiving to God" (2 Cor. 9:6–8, 11).

## Giving Helps Us Mature Spiritually

Giving to the Lord for the expansion of His kingdom breaks the iron grip money can have on our hearts. When we give, it increases our faith because we experience the effect our generosity has on others. They thank God for what He has used us to do. This stimulates us to more generosity and helps make us good role models for other believers. It's always faith-building to see the many ways God has of replenishing our supply.

Remember to keep this issue balanced: Money isn't bad. Possessions are not bad. They only become evil for us when they become our idols—the gods we give our lives to. Money is God's great rival.

# 12

## Pride's Subtle Masks

W HEN HELEN SHOWED UP for her appointment, she was quick to tell me she was both hurt and angry. Very angry. Her first words to me were, "How could children raised in our home, born into the fine family background we came from, have done this to us?"

Helen was well-manicured, nicely dressed, and held a respected place in the community. The firm set of her mouth and the regal arch of her eyebrows as she sat opposite me reflected tremendous pride. Not only was she proud of her family heritage, she also felt that she and her husband had done an excellent job of raising their children.

But Helen's children had chosen a lifestyle that horrified their parents—besides the tattoos and multiple earrings, a punk-rock band was headquartered in her sons' apartment, and she'd heard from the neighbors that girls had been seen coming and going at all hours. Helen refused to even entertain thoughts of drug or alcohol use—it was beyond her imagination that the story could get any worse than it already was.

Helen was deeply ashamed of the way her two boys had turned out. Her sense of worth had been wrapped up in raising children that were successful, according to *her* definition of success. If her boys had turned out the way she'd wanted them to, she would have felt affirmed as a mother and very proud of herself. Most likely she would also have quietly and condescendingly looked down on parents whose kids hadn't turned out quite as well as hers. Now she had no choice but to feel foolish, rejected, and angry.

Isn't this kind of emotional reaction a temptation for all of us?

## A Sense of Accomplishment

The truth is, some of the feelings of pride we experience aren't the least bit wrong or inappropriate. For example, how do you feel when . . .

- A dinner party you worked on for days turns out perfectly?
- Your child comes home with all A's on his or her report card?
- You get a merit raise at work?
- You move to a new, larger home?
- You are still able to get into your wedding dress on your twenty-fifth anniversary?
- Your children choose mates you approve of?
- You redecorate your living room and it looks great?

What is the feeling you have at these accomplishments?

Do you experience pleasure and a sense of satisfaction? Is it all right to feel that way? Here's the conclusion reached by Solomon, the wisest man, besides Jesus, who ever lived:

"Then I realized that it is good and proper for a man to eat and drink, and to find satisfaction in his toilsome labor under the sun during the few days of life God has given him—for this is his lot. Moreover when God gives any man wealth and possessions, and enables him to enjoy them, to accept his lot and be happy in his work—this is a gift of God" (Eccles. 5:18–19).

## Pride in Achievement

God wants us to take pleasure in our achievements. It's a gift from God to be able to work hard and see the tangible results of our efforts. God wants us to enjoy not only our accomplishments, but our work itself. In fact, it is gross ingratitude not to enjoy our work and what we accomplish through it. So what is the difference between this sense of satisfaction that contributes to a healthy self-esteem and the unhealthy pride that God hates?

Unhealthy pride, by definition, is an excessively high opinion of oneself. This results in a person's reputation, needs, desires, dignity, and public image being his or her main interest and concern, regardless of the effect on others.

Pleasure and satisfaction can slip over the edge and fall into pride when we think we are important or superior because of who we are, what we have, or what we have done. What happens when we fail to acknowledge that God is responsible for everything we are, have, and do in this life? A story in the Bible describes just such a scenario. It's a story about Uzziah, who was just sixteen when he became king of Judah. He was very successful in everything he did. We learn right away the reason for his success:

"He did what was right in the eyes of the LORD, just as his father Amaziah had done. He sought God during the days of Zechariah, who instructed him in the fear of God. As long as he sought the LORD, God gave him success" (2 Chron. 26:4–5).

Uzziah wanted to know God, and he put himself under the instruction of a prophet who taught him God's Word and God's ways. God responded by giving Uzziah success in every area of his life. He also gave him victory over Israel's ancient enemies, so that Uzziah became famous and very powerful.

Uzziah strengthened the defenses of Jerusalem. He improved grazing lands in the desert by building cisterns to catch the rainwater so that his livestock could flourish. He loved the soil and was an expert in agriculture. He had a well-trained, well-equipped army of 307,500 men to defend his country. "His fame spread far and wide, for he was greatly helped until he became powerful" (2 Chron. 26:15).

God gave this godly king the power to win his battles. God gave him wealth in livestock and abundant harvests. God used Uzziah as evidence to His people as well as to the nations all around that when a person worshiped the living God and obeyed His Word, he would be blessed in every way. But little by little, something happened to Uzziah. "After Uzziah became powerful, his pride led to his downfall" (2 Chron. 26:16).

## Pride Exalts Self and Forgets God

Uzziah's head had swelled with success. He somehow came to believe that his success was the result of his own ability and power and that he was a superior person. He forgot that God was the One who had helped and blessed him all along. He decided it wasn't enough simply to be king; He would take the religious leadership as well.

"Uzziah . . . was unfaithful to the LORD his God, and entered the temple of the LORD to burn incense on the altar of incense. Azariah the priest with eighty other courageous priests of the LORD followed him in" (2 Chron. 26:16b–18).

Uzziah was in direct defiance of God's specific instructions regarding the priesthood. Only descendants of Aaron could be priests and burn incense in the holy place. When Uzziah arrogantly walked into the temple with the censer in his hand, the high priest, with eighty others, blocked his way. Notice how Uzziah's act is described—"He was unfaithful to the Lord his God."

When he was rebuked, instead of repenting, he became infuriated and raged at the priests. Anger is often a symptom of pride that we display when our control is threatened and we can't have our own way. What would have happened in this situation if God had not intervened is anyone's guess!

"Uzziah, who had a censer in his hand ready to burn incense, became angry. While he was raging at the priests in their presence before the incense altar in the LORD's temple, leprosy broke out on his forehead. When Azariah the chief priest and all the other priests looked at him, they saw that he had leprosy on his forehead, so they hurried him out. Indeed, he himself was eager to leave, because the LORD had afflicted him" (2 Chron. 26:19–21).

*Leprosy!* And Uzziah didn't face a gradual case of the disease, but instantaneous symptoms that rendered him permanently unclean. He could never enter the temple again. He lived in quarantine until the day he died. Uzziah's son became co-regent with him and carried on the work of governing. Uzziah's power and glory were gone, and he was effectively king in name only. When he had decided he was a special person and the rules didn't apply to him, he had lost it all. The fact is, God hates pride. Eventually, He will humble the proud.

God was the One who had first exalted Uzziah, and God was the One who humbled him. Uzziah lost everything when he forgot that the reason for all his victory, power, and fame was obedience to God's Word and acknowledgment of His sovereignty.

Maybe you think God's punishment was too severe. But Jesus said, "To whom much is given, from him much will be required."[1] The punishment for those in leadership is usually much harsher because of their example and influence. "When pride comes, then comes disgrace, but with humility comes wisdom" (Prov. 11:2). "Pride goes before destruction, a haughty spirit before a fall" (Prov. 16:18).

Many years later, a proud pagan king learned the same lesson and expressed it well:

"Now, I, Nebuchadnezzar, praise and exalt and glorify the King of heaven, because everything he does is right and all his ways are just. And those who walk in pride he is able to humble" (Dan. 4:37).

## Pride Takes Credit For Prosperity

When we take all the credit for our accomplishments and forget that God is the One who has given us our ability, that's the kind of pride God hates. Think about it: Who gave you your intellectual capacity? If you graduated with honors, it's true that you worked hard, but another student may have worked even harder and not made it. Why? Different IQs.

Who gave you your physical makeup? If you have never had to struggle with keeping your weight down because you have "thin genes," do you think you're superior to the person who fights with fat every day of her life?

Who gave you the ability to make money and invest it well? Perhaps you have the Midas touch and it seems so easy. Do you look down on people who live from paycheck to paycheck even though they practice every economy?

Who gave you your personality? If you're an extrovert, do you think you're better than a shy, retiring person? Who gave you creativity and artistic ability? You can see ways to put flowers or words or musical notes together to create things of beauty. Others can't even figure out how you do it. Does that make you superior?

Who gave you the skills that have made you successful in your job or profession? Sure, you've been diligent. You've taken courses, sharpened your skills—but others have tried just as hard and not made the grade.

"Who makes you different from anyone else? What do you have that you did not receive? And if you did receive it, why do you boast as though you did not?" (1 Cor. 4:7).

Do you get the point? God claims the credit for creating us and for the blessings He showers on us. He wants us to give Him the glory and thank Him. That will keep us from the kind of pride and self-sufficiency that becomes a stench in His nostrils. "The LORD detests all the proud of heart. Be sure of this: They will not go unpunished" (Prov. 16:5).

## Satan's Proud Fall

Are you aware that pride was Satan's original sin? Here's how the prophet Isaiah described the great angel's fall: "How you have fallen from heaven, O morning star, son of the dawn! You have been cast down to the earth, you who once laid low the nations! You said in your heart, 'I will ascend to heaven; I will raise my throne above the stars of God; I will sit enthroned on the mount of assembly, on the utmost heights of the sacred mountain. I will ascend above the tops of the clouds; I will make myself like the Most High.' But you are brought down to the grave, to the depths of the pit" (Isa. 14:12–15).

It wasn't enough for Lucifer to be the highest-ranking cherub, filled with beauty and wisdom. He aspired to be like God, and that's exactly the bait he used to tempt Adam and Eve. He dangled the forbidden fruit before their eyes and said God didn't want them to eat it because then "they would be like God."

Pride and independence from God made our first parents sinners, and that prideful nature was passed on to the whole race. Do you see why God hates pride? It's the fertile ground for all other sins to flourish. We see this in the New Testament as well when Paul predicted what the last days before the Lord's return will be like. Listen and see if this doesn't sound like it could describe the subjects of the stories on today's ten o'clock news:

"But mark this: There will be terrible times in the last days. People will be lovers of themselves, lovers of money, boastful, proud, abusive, disobedient to their parents, ungrateful, unholy, without love, unforgiving, slanderous, without self-control, brutal, not lovers of the good, treacherous, rash, conceited, lovers of pleasure rather than lovers of God—having a form of godliness but denying its power. Have nothing to do with them" (2 Tim. 3:1–5).

Notice that the list starts with "lovers of themselves." That's a good overall definition of pride. Then there are other words: "boastful," "proud," "conceited." The Holy Spirit, who is the Author of Scripture, wants us to have a clear picture of what pride looks like, internally and externally. Look at the terrible emotions, attitudes, and conduct it produces: abusiveness, disobedience, ungratefulness, unholiness, without love, brutality, and so forth.

A teenager hires other teenagers to kill her parents.

Newborn babies are left in a dumpster.

A father sitting down with his family for a hamburger in a mall is killed before their eyes by a wild bullet because some gang members had a disagreement.

A bus driver is shot because a teenager objects to a seventy-five-cent fare.

Men, women, and children are killed in their homes and on the streets by drive-by shootings.

A maniac with a gun and a grievance mows down innocent people in a restaurant, a post office, and even a school.

Federal law permits and protects the slaughter of millions of unborn infants each year.

Sexual predators are viewed as needy people with a natural, unsatisfied hunger, not as sinners.

What more evidence do we need to prove that we are living in a culture that has forgotten God and His moral laws and exalted man? This kind of reprobation is the ultimate result of pride in the human heart. No wonder God hates it! James and Peter both quote Proverbs 3:34 to stress this point: "God opposes the proud but gives grace to the humble."[2]

When we read those indicting words in 1 Timothy, we are compelled to examine our hearts to see if any vestige of pride lurks there. How can we test ourselves so we can be honest and deal with this sin where we find it? Here are four key questions we should ask ourselves:

- Am I in competition with others?

- Do I feel I have to be self-sufficient?

- Do I struggle with my self-image?

- Do I choose my friends for their appearance, position, or performance?

Let's take a closer look at each of these questions.

## Am I in Competition with Others?

There's nothing wrong with wanting to do our best. But problems arise when we compare ourselves to others. Is she a better teacher than I am? Do I get a better salary? Is my home more expensive and attractive? Is my marriage happier? Are my children more obedient or successful? When our sense of worth and our evaluations of others are dependent on comparison and competition, pride is at the root.

"If anyone thinks he is something when he is nothing, he deceives himself. Each one should test his own actions. Then he can take pride in himself, without comparing himself to somebody else, for each one should carry his own load" (Gal. 6:3–5).

## Do I Feel I Have to Be Self-Sufficient?

When we have a problem, some of us share a basic misconception that we don't need anyone and we can make it alone. That's nothing but pride! God never intended for people to function that way. He especially never intended this for His redeemed people—His family!

It takes humility to let down our guard and ask for counsel. Or to allow others to help us out of a financial crisis. Or to accept help with meals in times of illness. We are all members of one body, and each part is essential and interdependent on others. If we believe this, it will help to cure us of pride.

## Do I Struggle with My Self-Image?

When we criticize someone else, is it an attempt to put ourselves in a superior position because we have concerns about our own inadequacy? Do we find ourselves boasting about ourselves? Pride is often a cover-up for insecurity. And a feeling of inferiority is often pride in reverse (more about that in the next chapter).

## Do I Choose My Friends for Their Appearance, Position, or Performance?

If we only want to be friends with people who are in our tax bracket and we make no effort to associate with those in more humble positions and occupations, that is pride. God simply forbids it for a believer. As Paul said, "Live in harmony with one another. Do not be proud, but be willing to associate with people of low position. Do not be conceited" (Rom. 12:16).

Paul wasn't the only one to speak out against pride. James also made some caustic remarks about snobbery.[3]

### Overcoming Pride

You may have identified with some of the questions I've asked here. We all have to keep close watch on our attitudes. If we don't recognize that pride is a constant temptation and repent of it, we will not go on to spiritual maturity to the measure God wants for us. Here are some practical suggestions for how we can control this problem:

## Don't Compare Yourself to Others

Don't compare yourself with other people or put one person into competition with another, evaluating their worth based on some standard you have selected. "We do not dare to classify or compare ourselves with some who commend themselves. When they measure themselves by themselves and compare themselves with themselves, they are not wise" (2 Cor. 10:12).

God wants us to accept people as they are, with all their good qualities as well as their less-attractive ones. Accept yourself the same way. Then when you see others succeed, you can be proud of them in an unselfish way. That's how Paul felt about the Corinthians, and he told them so, saying, "I have great confidence in you; I take great pride in you" (2 Cor. 7:4).

Can you imagine the difference it would make with our husbands, children, and friends if instead of criticizing them we told them we were proud of them? We'd help them develop a healthy self-image instead of continuously trying to build up ourselves.

## Desire God's Will More Than Your Own

The proud person wants to be in control. That's why obedience to this verse is a sure cure for pride. Submission to God doesn't leave much room for personal arrogance. "And what does the LORD require of you but to do justly, to love mercy, and to walk humbly with your God" (Mic. 6:8).

Learn to pray in humility, "Lord, I want Your will more than my own way. If You want me to be rich, influential, or famous, I'll trust You. But if You want me to simply walk with You in faithfulness and obscurity, I'll trust You to use me wherever You place me. All I want is Your will for my life." Humility with God forces us to be humble with one another.

## Accept God's Unconditional Love

God wants us to have a balanced, healthy self-image because we believe two things. First, we believe He created us to be image-bearers of God. Second, we believe He loves us so much that He gave His own Son to save us and reconcile us to Himself.

Every person who has trusted in Jesus Christ is a child of God. We don't have to earn His love by our own efforts. God doesn't love us because we are lovable but because it's His nature to love. He just loves us as we are. If we really believe this, we will have a healthy, balanced self-image that comes from humility, not from pride.

## Develop the Quality of Humility

"Humility is defined as a modest sense of one's own importance. It includes a courteous nature and a deep respect for the dignity of all humans."[4]

Jesus is our greatest example. He left the glories of heaven to come to earth and live life as a human being for thirty-three years. He humbled Himself to die a criminal's death on the cross for our salvation. And He invites us to come to Him and learn from Him: "Come to me, all you who are weary and burdened, and I will give you rest. Take my yoke upon you and learn from me, for I am gentle and humble in heart, and you will find rest for your souls" (Matt. 11:28–29).

Jesus will give us rest from the burden of preoccupation with ourselves, our self-image, our reputation, our feelings of superiority or inferiority. He will teach us to be gentle and humble—to have a realistic evaluation of ourselves and to be grateful for who we are and where we are. His Spirit will cultivate these qualities in us as we give up our pride and independence and come to Jesus for deliverance and rest.

If you have never put your trust in the Lord Jesus Christ to save you, wouldn't today be a great time to begin a new life—life as a forgiven child of God? It takes humility to confess that you are a sinner and can't earn God's favor. Don't let pride keep you from a relationship with God.

Jeremiah sums it up well: "This is what the LORD says: 'Let not the wise man boast of his wisdom or the strong man boast of his strength or the rich man boast of his riches, but let him who boasts boast about this: that he understands and knows me, that I am the LORD, who exercises kindness, justice and righteousness on earth, for in these I delight'" (Jer. 9:23–24).

# 13

### Inferiority—Another
### Form of Pride?

YOU'RE AT A FRIEND'S DINNER PARTY. As you seat yourself at the table, you can't help but notice the festive centerpiece, the matching plates and napkins, the elegant place cards. The meal is presented beautifully, and the food looks and tastes wonderful. As for you, no matter how hard you try, you never can get a table to look even slightly attractive. Worse yet, your cooking is mediocre, to say the least.

*How do you feel?*

You had a college roommate who talked to her boyfriend on the phone for three hours every night, cut classes, and simply breezed through her homework with hardly any studying. She got straight A's and graduated magna cum laude. Meanwhile, you had to study several hours a night for every B you got.

*How did you feel?*

Several of the women in your Bible study work out at the gym three times a week. After the study, they change their clothes in the church restroom and head for the fitness center looking slim and trendy in their pastel Lycra tights. Once at the center, they excel in every area of physical prowess. When you decide to join them, you have to wear a huge T-shirt to cover your bulging tummy and thighs, and you can hardly do one push-up without falling flat.

*How does that make you feel?*

You have a pretty, stylish neighbor who is organized and efficient. She is friendly, chatty, and no matter how many things she has to do, she gets the job done while looking perfectly groomed in the process. Her house is always immaculate, her kids are always obedient, and she never has so much as a broken fingernail. In contrast, your family seems like a fragmented, disorderly, and inefficient group of savages.

*How does this woman make you feel?*

If these kinds of comparisons make you feel inferior, it's because you're making two mistakes:

First, it is a mistake to measure anyone's worth by appearance or performance.

Second, it is a mistake to compare ourselves to others.

When these two errors are in effect, we always have a shifting, unstable view of our own value. Without exception, there will always be someone who can outdo us at something.

## Why Do We Feel So Inferior?

Inferiority is a persistent sense of inadequacy or a tendency to underrate oneself and one's abilities. Most of us don't have too much trouble recognizing the "symptoms" brought about by feelings of inferiority. But do we know why those feelings are at work? There are three typical causes of inferior feelings: consistent disapproval, unbalanced approval, and being habitually controlled.

### Consistent Disapproval

Some people received negative messages throughout their childhood. Maybe you were told you were an unwanted baby. Or you were seldom praised for your accomplishments. Of, if you came home with all A's and one B, instead of praise for the A's, the question was, "Why didn't you get A in this subject too?" If a person is never able to please his or her parents, it's easy to grow up with feelings of inferiority.

### Unbalanced Approval

On the other hand, if you were only told how wonderful and superior you are, then feelings of inferiority surface when you recognize your own weaknesses. You know down deep inside that you aren't superior but just average, and you feel like you're deceiving everyone. We need positive input, but it must be realistic and balanced. No one is absolutely perfect in every way.

### Being Controlled

A person can develop feelings of inferiority if he or she has been controlled by someone consistently for a long period of time. Your mother or father may have been critical and controlling. Your husband may have given you the message that you can't do anything right. Somewhere along the way, a teacher or a coach may have had a negative effect on you.

# Inferiority—Another Form of Pride?

## Questions about Inadequacy

Whatever the causes of your feelings, if you allow them to control you, a sense of inferiority will keep you from exploring and achieving the wonderful goals God has for you. How can you tell if that is happening? Consider the following questions:

- When your plans don't work out, do you get easily discouraged and consider it a personal failure?

- Are you plagued with doubts about your ability? Do you constantly think "I can't do it!"?

- Do you hide your feelings by acting arrogant or superior when you feel challenged or threatened?

- Do you get angry when things don't go your way?

- Are you rigid and inflexible, resistant to change?

We are all vulnerable to inferior feelings at some time or other, but we don't have to let them take up permanent residence in our lives. God has made each of us unique, different from everyone else, with both superior and inferior skills. Our capabilities, however, have nothing to do with the intrinsic value God has placed on us. When Jesus was here on earth, He welcomed all sorts of people—fishermen, tax collectors, prostitutes, housewives, rulers, and the rich and the poor. He died for each one of us. God's price tag on us will never change, no matter how skillful or unskillful we are. Each of us is a one-of-a-kind person, and we will never be less valuable or more valuable to God than we are right now.

## Jeremiah—A Prophet Who Felt Inadequate

I'm so grateful that the Bible draws accurate pictures of its characters. If they were all heroic and perfect without any self-doubt or failure, we wouldn't be able to relate to them at all. One man in the Bible expressed his emotions, his fears, his inadequacies, and his doubts more than anyone else in Scripture, except David in the Psalms. He is the prophet Jeremiah. We learn a lot about Jeremiah and his times in the first few verses of his book. He was from a priestly family although he never served as a priest.

Josiah the king, who had ascended to the throne of Judah when he was only eight years old, was in the thirteenth year of his reign. When Josiah was sixteen, he had begun to seek God and serve Him, and when he was twenty he began to purge the land of all the symbols and trappings of idolatry.

Josiah tore down the pagan altars and smashed the idols and images throughout the land. He was the last good and godly king Judah had, but even his reforms could not prevent God's promised judgment on His people. They had gone too far. Within forty years they would be destroyed as a nation and carried into exile—Israel already had been swept into captivity one hundred years before. But the Lord was pleased with Josiah and his desire to turn his nation back to the living God, so He provided an ally, a man who would preach God's Word to a rebellious people.

In Josiah's thirteenth year, in the midst of his reforms, something extraordinary happened to young Jeremiah. God revealed His plan for Jeremiah's life and gave him a ministry that would last for forty-four years. Here's what the Lord said to Jeremiah: "Before I formed you in the womb I knew you, before you were born I set you apart; I appointed you as a prophet to the nations" (Jer. 1:5).

The word *knew* is used in other Scriptures to indicate a close personal relationship; thus it describes someone who is chosen and protected. Before Jeremiah was conceived, God intended to have a close relationship with him. While he was still in the womb, God set him apart for His exclusive use. God appointed him to be a prophet to the nations.

### Jeremiah's Mission-Impossible

What a shock God's message was to young Jeremiah! A prophet was a person through whom God spoke directly to His people. Jeremiah was overwhelmed with his assignment. He said, "Ah, Sovereign LORD, . . . I do not know how to speak; I am only a child" (Jer. 1:6).

The young man was probably in his late teens or early twenties. Do you hear his feelings of inferiority and inadequacy? All through his book, you will find that Jeremiah is very honest about his feelings. He was a timid, gentle, sensitive, emotional young man on whom God had laid His hand for a specific purpose. God immediately answered Him: "Do not say 'I am only a child.' You must go to everyone I send you to and say whatever I command you. Do not be afraid of them, for I am with you and will rescue you" (Jer. 1:7).

What happened next must have been truly astonishing. Jeremiah said, "Then the LORD reached out his hand and touched my mouth and said to me, 'Now, I have put my words in your mouth. See, today I appoint you over nations and kingdoms to uproot and tear down, to destroy and overthrow, to build and to plant'" (Jer. 1:7–10).

God told Jeremiah three important things here that would sustain him for the rest of his life. These same principles can help us find the confidence we need to overcome our own sense of inadequacy:

## He Was under God's Authority

Jeremiah did not have to work on sermons or solicit speaking invitations. God would send him where he wanted him to go, and God would tell him the words to say.

## He Was Protected by God's Presence

God told Jeremiah, "Do not be afraid of them." The reason Jeremiah didn't have to fear anyone was because God had promised His constant presence and protection, assuring him, "I will be with you and will rescue you." God didn't say Jeremiah would not be persecuted. In fact, He implies that he will. But no one can destroy a person God promises to protect.

## God Was the Source of His Ability

In his vision, Jeremiah saw God reach out and touch his mouth to symbolically demonstrate that he was now God's spokesman. His feelings of inadequacy and inferiority were justified in his own strength, but the Lord made it clear to him that He would give him the ability and the power to do the job he was being commissioned to do.

Next, the Lord told Jeremiah the messages he would bring: Jeremiah was to preach judgment and restoration. Jeremiah was not going to be a popular preacher! His messages would be more negative than positive. Notice the four negative actions God mentioned: "Uproot," "tear down," "destroy," and "overthrow." There were only two positives: "build" and "plant."

## Visions of Destruction

God followed up this summary of what Jeremiah was to do with two visions that illustrated and confirmed what He had said. He then told Jeremiah the meaning of each vision:

"'What do you see, Jeremiah?'

"'I see the branch of an almond tree,' I replied.

"The LORD said to me, 'You have seen correctly, for I am watching to see that my word is fulfilled.'

"The word of the LORD came to me again: 'What do you see?'

"'I see a boiling pot, tilting away from the north,' I answered.

"The LORD said to me, 'From the north disaster will be poured out on all who live in the land. I am about to summon all the peoples of the northern kingdoms,' declares the LORD" (Jer. 1:11–15).

The Lord was watching to see that His Word was fulfilled. He was in complete control. Judah would be overrun and conquered by a foreign enemy because God's people had forsaken Him and worshiped idols.

Every time Jeremiah stood up to preach, people would hear about the terrible judgment that was coming because of their sins. But Jeremiah would tell them God would not utterly reject them; one day, he would say, they would be restored as a nation. Despite their "happy endings," these messages were not going to win Jeremiah many friends. In fact, they would make him many powerful enemies.

Knowing this, God told Jeremiah, "Get yourself ready! Stand up and say to them whatever I command you. Do not be terrified by them, or I will terrify you before them. Today I have made you a fortified city, an iron pillar and a bronze wall to stand against the whole land—against the kings of Judah, its officials, its priests and the people of the land. They will fight against you but will not overcome you, for I am with you and will rescue you" (Jer. 1:17–19).

## Jeremiah Had God's Guarantee—His Promises

I'm sure this was not the kind of future Jeremiah had looked forward to; it didn't sound very much like "God loves you and has a wonderful plan for your life." He must have been overwhelmed with a sense of inadequacy. But he was obedient to God's commission, and over the years, he faithfully did the job God called him to do.

It wasn't an easy life. People plotted against him, falsely accused him, tried to shut him up, even attempted to kill him. He was often discouraged and depressed. He wept, he complained, and he accused God of deceiving him, but no matter how he felt he always came back to the promises God had made to him at his call.

## Fighting Inferiority by Believing God's Promises

God had chosen Jeremiah to be His prophet, so he was acting under God's authority and with His power. And he depended on God to protect him. He had God's guarantee, His promises. God kept His promises and made Jeremiah a powerful prophet for the rest of his life. He will do no less for you and for me if we honor His principles.

## God Has Chosen Us, and He Will Be with Us

From Jeremiah we learn something very important for ourselves: When God gives us a task, He gives us the ability to do it. He provides the encouragement and the help we need to persevere.

Suppose Jeremiah had been so focused on his youth, inexperience, and feelings of inadequacy that he had disobeyed God. It could have happened to him, and it can happen to us. If we let feelings of inferiority or inadequacy control us, we'll cheat ourselves of the great achievements and blessings we could otherwise have.

Some of the most effective people in history experienced feelings of inadequacy, but they persevered in spite of it. The great apostle Paul spoke and wrote with great authority. But he knew he was not adequate in himself to do what God called him to do. He said, "But thanks be to God, who always leads us in triumphal procession in Christ and through us spreads everywhere the fragrance of the knowledge of him. For we are to God the aroma of Christ among those who are perishing. To the one we are the smell of death; to the other, the fragrance of life. And who is equal to such a task?" (2 Cor. 2:14–16).

The picture here is of a conquering general enjoying his victory parade. Jesus Christ is the Victor leading us "in triumphal procession," and we who have trusted Him are victors with Him. God will use us to spread the knowledge of Him, like a sweet perfume, to everyone. People will make decisions based on our message. Some will believe and join us in the parade. Some will reject the Savior.

God has given to us the awesome responsibility of living and giving the good news of salvation to a hungry world. Paul expressed what most of us feel when we consider that task. He asked, "And who is equal to such a task? J. B. Phillips translates it, "Who could think himself adequate for a responsibility like this?"[1]

None of us feels competent in ourselves to live the Christian life in a way that will win others to Christ. No one is adequate to preach and teach and serve the Lord in a way that will make an eternal impact on other people. We can't do a supernatural work in our natural strength.

## God Is the Source of Our Competence

Actually, feeling inadequate is exactly what we all should feel, because then we'll depend on the Lord to make us competent. As Paul said, "Such confidence as this is ours through Christ before God. Not that we are competent in ourselves to claim anything for ourselves, but our competence comes from God" (2 Cor. 3:4–5).

Jesus said, "Apart from me you can do nothing!" (John 15:5). His Holy Spirit lives within us. The same Person who empowered the Lord Jesus in His ministry is in residence in our hearts. He opens God's Word to us. He motivates us to obey it. He puts His thoughts into our minds. He gives us the words to say and gives them supernatural power. He invests every act of service and obedience with eternal value and impact.

Paul's letter to the Philippians encourages us further: "For it is God who works in you to will and to act according to his good purpose. . . . I can do everything through him who gives me strength" (Phil. 2:13 and 4:13).

God is the One who makes us want to do His will, and He gives us the ability to perform it. We can depend on our loving Savior for strength; He never gets tired or impatient with us.

## We Are Protected by God's Presence

The Lord promises His constant presence in our lives. He said, "Never will I leave you; never will I forsake you" (Heb. 13:5).

Nothing can happen to us that isn't sifted through His hands. We don't have to be crippled by fear. Fear of other people, fear of personal failure, fear of the future—none of these fears has any place in the life of God's chosen child.

## God Gives Us His Promises As Our Guarantee

There is a secret to finding spiritual victory over feelings of inadequacy and inferiority: *faith*. Faith reminds us that God is trustworthy and able to do what He says He will do. By an act of your will, you can choose faith over inferiority. Ask yourself these questions:

- Do you suffer from feelings of inferiority and inadequacy?

- Do you feel inferior because of the family you came from?

- Do you lack confidence about your social skills?

- Do you feel inferior because you don't have a pretty face or perfect figure?

- Do you feel inadequate for the challenges of your job?

- Does the responsibility of raising your children to be good and godly stress you out?

- Do you doubt your ability to contribute to a lasting marriage?

- Do you feel incapable of making and keeping friends?

- Are you afraid if you offer to serve in the community or church you will fail?

- Do you feel guilty that you don't speak up for the Lord when you could because you aren't sure what to say?

If you have yes answers to any of these questions, you have a wonderful adventure ahead of you! Tell God exactly how you feel. Tell Him you are helpless to change, but you are willing to trust Him to make you competent to handle the responsibilities of your life. Then depend on Him all day long and see how He meets your need.

## Victory over Fear of Inadequacy Is Won by Faith

There's nothing wrong with feeling inadequate from time to time. It happens to everyone, and those feelings should drive us toward dependence on the Lord to make us competent. But if we simply accept our inadequacy as an unchangeable fact, we develop an inferiority complex that will hinder us all our lives.

When we act with our will to believe God's promises to us, to acknowledge Him as the source of our abilities, to trust that He will make us adequate for all the circumstances of life, then we will have victory over feelings of inferiority and inadequacy that stand as obstacles to our growth to emotional, social, and spiritual maturity.

# 14

## Dealing with Disappointment

ALICE HAD HUGE, BROWN EYES and a sweet voice that made me think of a little girl. She wanted to talk to me, she had explained, because of a recent physical problem she'd experienced.

"What kind of a physical problem, Alice?"

She stared at me for a moment, trying to find the right answer. Finally, with tears in her eyes, she said just one word: "Miscarriages . . ."

"How many, Alice?"

"Three. The third one was a week ago . . ."

After that, Alice was unable to speak for a few minutes. When she finally did, she was full of hard questions. "Vickie, how can you say God loves me when He never answers my prayers? The one thing I want most in the world is a baby. Is that too much to ask?"

"God loves you, Alice. There's no doubt about that."

"But if He loved me, wouldn't He see how much pain I'm in? How much pain Tom is in? We want a baby more than anything, and we'd be godly, loving parents. Yet, when you look around, everyone else gets pregnant. Everyone! People who don't even want babies get pregnant and then kill them in abortions. I've promised the Lord I would quit my job and care for my child. I'd teach it to know the Lord. It's just so unfair. We pray and pray, and God doesn't hear our prayers!"

## The Shadow of Disappointment

Disappointment comes in all sizes, doesn't it? Any time our hopes are not realized or our expectations or desires are not fulfilled, we feel disappointed. Disappointment can be a passing emotion over a temporary loss, or it may strike powerfully when something permanently changes our lives. A major disappointment can remain within us all the time, shadowing our reactions to everything.

We all experience disappointment for different reasons. In itself, feeling disappointed is not a sin. How we handle it is the crucial issue. Disappointment is so common to humanity that it was difficult to choose which biblical characters to best illustrate it. The Bible is full of disappointed people!

Think of the years of disappointment experienced by Sarah, Rebekah, Rachel, Hannah, and Elizabeth. Month after month, year after year, they saw the evidence of their childlessness. Job and Joseph had good reason to be disappointed, too, both in people and in God. Elijah the prophet expected the great evidence of God's power on Mount Carmel would bring revival. Instead, it only put a price on his head. He was so disappointed he asked to die.

## Moses—A Man Who Understood Disappointment

If anyone was ever faced with a repeated disappointment, it was Moses. In infancy he was rescued from death by the faith of his parents and the ingenuity of his mother. God arranged for him to be adopted by the princess of Egypt. But he spent the first formative years of his life being raised by his own parents. From them he learned of God's promises to Abraham, Isaac, and Jacob. He was taught that the Israelites were God's people, chosen to bless the world, and that God would make them a nation and give them a land.

Moses was never able to forget what his parents had taught him, even after he went to live with Pharaoh's daughter, his foster mother, in the palace. This double identity must have caused him a great deal of tension. As he grew, he saw the Hebrew slaves struggling under terrible bondage while he lived luxuriously, enjoying all the privileges of royalty. Finally, Moses tried to do something to help his people.

"When Moses was forty years old, he decided to visit his fellow Israelites. He saw one of them being mistreated by an Egyptian, so he went to his defense and avenged him by killing the Egyptian. Moses thought that his own people would realize that God was using him to rescue them, but they did not" (Acts 7:23–25).

Many years before God called him to do so, Moses longed to be a deliverer of his people. He was willing to use his power and influence to change their desperate situation. But they rejected him. In fact, he had to flee for his life from Egypt to live in the backside of the desert for another forty years after the murder incident. Talk about disappointment!

## Two Key Reasons for Disappointment

Moses had two reasons to be disappointed. First, he was disappointed in people—because his expectations that his people would understand what he wanted to do for them and would accept him were not fulfilled.

Second, he was disappointed in his circumstances. After years of privilege and education in Egypt, he certainly had never dreamed that he would spend the rest of his life tending sheep in a desert. What a discouraging future!

Today, we become disappointed for precisely the same two reasons. When we set our hearts on *people* or on *circumstances*, we are usually disappointed. God wants us to set our hearts only on Him. He wants us to trust in His goodness, even in the midst of our deepest disappointments.

Moses was leading a flock of sheep around the Sinai wilderness when God spoke to him from the burning bush. What a shock it was to hear that *this* was the time for him to do what he had once wanted to do—to deliver his people from Egypt.

"The LORD said, 'I have indeed seen the misery of my people in Egypt. I have heard them crying out because of their slave drivers, and I am concerned about their suffering. So I have come down to rescue them from the hand of the Egyptians and to bring them up out of that land into a good and spacious land, a land flowing with milk and honey. . . . And now the cry of the Israelites has reached me, and I have seen the way the Egyptians are oppressing them. So now, go. I am sending you to Pharaoh to bring my people the Israelites out of Egypt.'

"But Moses said to God, 'Who am I, that I should go to Pharaoh and bring the Israelites out of Egypt?'

"And God said, 'I will be with you. And this will be the

sign to you that it is I who have sent you: When you have brought the people out of Egypt, you will worship God on this mountain'" (Exod. 3:7–8a, 9–12).

Despite the thrilling experience of hearing God's voice coming from the burning bush, all of Moses' self-confidence was gone. For the rest of Exodus 3 and half of Exodus 4, God patiently answered each of Moses' objections and insecurities. He promised to be with him. He gave him the power to perform miracles. He assured him that the Israelites would follow him this time and that God would compel the Egyptians to let them go by His great power.

But Moses was a discouraged and defeated man. Even God's wonderful promises didn't convince him.

"Moses said to the LORD, 'O LORD, I have never been eloquent, neither in the past nor since you have spoken to your servant. I am slow of speech and tongue.'

"The LORD said to him, 'Who gave man his mouth? Who makes him deaf or mute? Who gives him sight or makes him blind? Is it not I, the LORD? Now go: I will help you speak and will teach you what to say.'

"But Moses said, 'O LORD, please send someone else to do it'" (Exod. 4:10–13).

This time God was angry; nevertheless He agreed to allow Moses' brother Aaron to accompany him and be his mouthpiece. Then Moses and Aaron told the elders about Israel God's message.

"Moses and Aaron brought together all the elders of the Israelites, and Aaron told them everything the LORD had said to Moses. He also performed the signs before the people, and they believed. And when they heard that the LORD was concerned about them and had seen their misery, they bowed down and worshiped" (Exod. 4:29–31).

This time the people accepted him and worshiped God, and Moses was encouraged. Things were working out as God had said they would. Now it was time to tell Pharaoh.

"Afterward Moses and Aaron went to Pharaoh and said, 'This is what the LORD, the God of Israel, says: "Let my people go, so that they may hold a festival to me in the desert."'

"Pharaoh said, 'Who is the LORD, that I should obey him and let Israel go? I do not know the LORD and I will not let Israel go'" (Exod. 5:1–2).

With these words, the battle lines were drawn between God and Pharaoh. Pharaoh oppressed his slaves even more, until life became unbearable for them. And who was to blame? Moses, of course.

"When they left Pharaoh, they found Moses and Aaron waiting to meet them, and they said, 'May the LORD look upon you and judge you! You have made us a stench to Pharaoh and his officials and have put a sword in their hand to kill us'" (Exod. 5:20–21).

Can you imagine the disappointment Moses felt when he heard their words? He had told them God would deliver them. Instead, their circumstances were worse than ever. Naturally, Moses was disappointed too. But in handling his disappointment he showed us what to do when our own expectations are not realized.

"Moses returned to the LORD and said, 'O Lord, why have you brought trouble upon this people? Is this why you sent me? Ever since I went to Pharaoh to speak in your name, he has brought trouble upon this people, and you have not rescued your people at all'" (Exod. 5:22–23).

Moses blamed God for all the trouble. He accused God of not keeping His promises. But the important thing is that he came to God and expressed his doubts, fears, and feelings. God can handle that; He knows how we're feeling anyway. When we honestly tell Him of our disappointments and heartaches, He can reassure and comfort us and give us strength to go on.

"Then the LORD said to Moses, 'Now you will see what I will do to Pharaoh: Because of my mighty hand he will let them go; because of my mighty hand he will drive them out of his country' . . .

"But Moses said to the LORD, 'If the Israelites will not listen to me, why would Pharaoh listen to me, since I speak with faltering lips?'" (Exod. 6:1, 12).

Poor Moses! He was in the pits! He was depending on his own ability instead of realizing that he was simply the instrument in God's hands. God would accomplish the deliverance of his people, not Moses. His faith had a lot of growing to do, and God was very patient. He let him suffer disappointments because they drove him to know God, enabling Moses to trust Him to a greater degree. Of course, He does the same with us.

We're all familiar with this story describing how God displayed his mighty power in the devastating plagues that ruined Egypt. Ultimately, on that first Passover night, while the Egyptians mourned the deaths of their firstborn, Israel marched triumphantly out of the land of their long and cruel bondage.

God opened the Red Sea for them to pass on dry ground. In the days that followed, He led them with a pillar of cloud and fire. He fed them with manna. He gave them water from the rock. He supplied their every need. The Israelites heard God's voice at Sinai when He gave them His law to live by.

But over and over, the people complained. They were

disappointed about one thing and then another. Even though Moses increased in his faith and dependence on God, the people's constant griping drained his strength. In Numbers 11 they complained about the monotony of eating manna every day. Again, Moses was disappointed and discouraged.

"Moses heard the people of every family wailing, each at the entrance to his tent. The LORD became exceedingly angry, and Moses was troubled. He asked the LORD, 'Why have you brought this trouble on your servant? What have I done to displease you that you put the burden of all these people on me? Did I conceive all these people? Did I give them birth? Why do you tell me to carry them in my arms, as a nurse carries an infant, to the land you promised on oath to their forefathers? Where can I get meat for all these people? They keep wailing to me, "Give us meat to eat!" I cannot carry all these people by myself; the burden is too heavy for me. If this is how you are going to treat me, put me to death right now—if I have found favor in your eyes—and do not let me face my own ruin'" (Num. 11:10–15).

Moses was worn out. Instead of a grateful, joyful people, willing to endure anything to get to the wonderful homeland God had promised, he had to play nursemaid to a bunch of babies who were never satisfied, no matter what he or God did.

Do you ever feel disappointed and exhausted with the mundane routines of life? There is such monotony of doing the same thing every day: the meals, the carpool, the kids, the laundry, the shopping, the housecleaning. Do you have a job that is far below the skills you trained for? Do you have aged parents to care for, to the point that your own activities have had to be severely curtailed? Are your children demanding and too young to appreciate your efforts?

God recognizes genuine stress and will help us. Look at the way God relieved Moses:

"The LORD said to Moses: 'Bring me seventy of Israel's elders who are known to you as leaders and officials among the people. Have them come to the Tent of Meeting, that they may stand there with you. I will come down and speak with you there, and I will take of the Spirit that is on you and put the Spirit on them. They will help you carry the burden of the people so that you will not have to carry it alone'" (Num. 11:16–17).

First, God gave Moses seventy men to help him carry the burden of all these people. He didn't punish him; He helped him. God still uses other people to encourage and help us. But God wasn't finished. He told Moses to tell the Israelites, "Consecrate yourselves in preparation for tomorrow, when you will eat meat. The LORD heard you when you wailed, 'If only we had meat to eat! We were better off in Egypt!' Now the LORD will give you meat, and you will eat it. You will not eat it for just one day, or two days, or five, ten or twenty days, but for a whole month—until it comes out of your nostrils and you loathe it—because you have rejected the LORD, who is among you, and have wailed before him saying 'Why did we ever leave Egypt?'" (Num. 11:18–20).

God gave the people the change in diet they craved. But He showed His displeasure about their constant complaining and ingratitude by sending death with the quail He provided. For many, their first bite of quail was the last thing they ever ate.

## Moses's Final Disappointment

Moses wasn't through with disappointments. How his

heart must have broken when the people refused to go into the Promised Land because of the bad report of the ten spies. When God punished them with thirty-eight more years in the wilderness, Moses had to endure it with them, even though he had wanted to go forward and possess the land.

His worst and final disappointment came when he was forbidden to enter the land himself. This happened because of an outburst of pride and anger. He begged God to allow him to go across the Jordan. After all, hadn't he been a faithful servant for forty years? But God's answer was a resounding "No."

"The LORD was angry with me and would not listen to me. 'That is enough,' the LORD said. 'Do not speak to me anymore about this matter'" (Deut. 3:26).

Imagine God forbidding Moses even to pray about it anymore! Moses had to be satisfied with a bird's-eye view of the land from a mountain before he died, but he did not lead his people into it. There are some circumstances that will never change. We have to learn to accept them and to keep trusting God in spite of our disappointment. Only in doing so are we able to experience life at its fullest.

## David and Disappointment

Like Moses, David also experienced grave disappointment. When he was a teenager, God ordered the prophet Samuel to anoint David to be the next king of Israel. God had rejected Saul as king and had told him that none of his sons would be king after him. David's great victory over Goliath vaulted him into the limelight, and King Saul made him a military commander.

As David's popularity grew, Saul's fear and jealousy that

David might be his replacement also increased. Saul was determined to thwart God's revealed will and kill David, so David had to flee for his life. He was a fugitive from Saul for about ten years.

There were times when his discouragement was so acute that David's faith in the future that God had promised him vanished. He consequently did things that were wrong and foolish. At one point, he even pretended to have lost his mind. Another time, he tried to run away and hide among Israel's enemies.

"David thought to himself, 'One of these days I will be destroyed by the hand of Saul. The best thing I can do is to escape to the land of the Philistines. Then Saul will give up searching for me anywhere in Israel, and I will slip out of his hand.'

"So David and the six hundred men with him left and went over to Achish son of Maoch king of Gath. David and his men settled in Gath with Achish. Each man had his family with him, and David had his two wives: Ahinoam of Jezreel and Abigail of Carmel, the widow of Nabal. When Saul was told that David had fled to Gath, he no longer searched for him" (1 Sam. 27:1–4).

To be safe in the land of his enemies, David had to play the role of a traitor to Israel. Worse, he had to deceive and lie to his host. David wavered between discouragement and faith, just as we all do. He didn't understand God's timing. He didn't understand why he had to be on the run for his life when he had always been loyal to his king. Going to the enemy was not the right solution. But that's what he chose to do.

Sometimes God's way of doing things is really difficult for us. If He would only keep the schedule we've laid out for ourselves! If He cooperated, we wouldn't have doubts or disappointments. Of course the truth is that the most important time for our faith to be sturdy is precisely when we are disappointed and confused about what God is doing. Despite David's lapses, God did for him exactly what He had promised, and when he was thirty the throne was his. He wrote the Eighteenth Psalm after he had been delivered from all his enemies:

> I love you, O LORD, my strength.
> The LORD is my rock, my fortress and my deliverer;
> my God is my rock, in whom I take refuge.
> He is my shield and the horn of my salvation, my stronghold.
> I call to the LORD, who is worthy of praise,
> > and I am saved from my enemies. (Ps. 18:1–3)

It's easy to look back and praise God for what He has done. But true faith believes ahead of time what can only be seen by looking back.

## Disappointed Disciples

Disappointment among God's people wasn't limited to the Old Testament. Jesus' disciples also knew what it was to be keenly disappointed. They had fervently believed that Jesus was the Messiah, and they expected Him to usher in the Messianic kingdom. Instead, He was crucified and buried. And all their hopes were buried with Him in that tomb.

The disciples expected Israel to be rescued from Roman oppression when the Messiah came. Instead, the One on whom they had set their hearts died a criminal's death on a Roman cross. Listen to how Jesus scolded them for doubting Him.

"He said to them, 'How foolish you are, and how slow of heart to believe all that the prophets have spoken! Did not the Christ have to suffer these things and then enter his glory?' And beginning with Moses and all the Prophets, he explained to them what was said in all the Scriptures concerning himself" (Luke 24:25–27).

God had a much bigger plan that the Old Testament foretold. Jesus died and rose again to rescue all humanity from the bondage and oppression of sin. His redemption was not just to bring about a local and temporal change in earthly circumstances but a change in their eternal destiny. Did you ever think that Jesus can be disappointed with us? He was obviously disappointed with His disciples and their unbelief.

## Disappointment: The First Seed of Doubt

Disappointment is the first seed of doubt that intrudes on our faith. Disappointment sounds so harmless, but it's the tip of a wedge that will stop our spiritual growth and make us bitter and defeated (more about that soon). Think of disappointment as a test permitted by God to see if you'll continue trusting Him, obeying Him, and believing that He is good. That brings us back to those two sources of most disappointment: people and circumstances.

### Has a Person Disappointed You?

When we place our expectations on people, we are usually disappointed. Has a close friend turned away from you? Has someone betrayed you? If you have set your hopes on your children being all you want them to be, you could be headed for a huge letdown. Did you marry, thinking your husband would meet all your needs? I have to tell you something: No man can meet all of a woman's needs, and no woman can meet all of a man's needs. God made us with a vacant space in our innermost being that only He can fill. So He will always let us experience disappointment with people so that we are driven to find fulfillment in Him.

## Are You Disappointed in Your Circumstances?

If our joy depends on circumstances, we are in trouble, because circumstances are always changing. There are too many variables for them to remain the same. Did you expect a promotion, and someone less qualified got the job instead? Has illness interrupted and permanently altered the plans you had for your family? Has a divorce you never wanted radically changed your circumstances? Disappointment works in our lives like the wedge illustrated in Figure 14-1.[1]

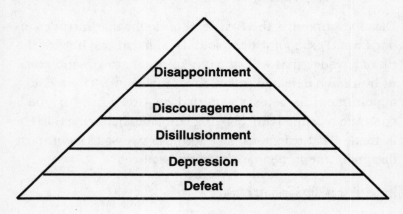

**Figure 14-1.**

Satan has a strategy to invade our spirits and bring us down until we are defeated. The tip of the wedge seems so harmless. It is simply *disappointment*.

But if we let our disappointment fester, the wedge is driven in a little farther, and we experience *discouragement*.

Unchecked, discouragement because *disillusionment*.

Then the wedge invades even more territory as it proceeds to *depression*.

Ultimately, we end in *defeat*.

How do we prevent the penetration of this deadly wedge into our spirits? We find the answer in 1 Thessalonians 5:18: "Give thanks in all circumstances."

## Thanksgiving—the Antidote to Disappointment

No matter what we are going through, we can find something to be thankful for. First and foremost, we can be thankful because we belong to God. If we have trusted Jesus Christ, God is our heavenly Father. He knows everything we are going through, and He is the only one in the universe who can make bad things work together for our good. So we can thank Him for His presence, His love, His blessings. We can rejoice that He has good plans for our future and that we receive His daily care, no matter how dark our circumstances seem.

Take another look at the wedge in Figure 14-1, and you'll see that the best place to give thanks is at the *disappointment* level. If we break the progression there, we won't go on to experience the other emotions that stunt our spiritual growth and drag us down to defeat.

We have to learn what the writer of the Seventy-third Psalm learned. When he contemplated the injustice all around him, the success of the wicked, and the troubles of the righteous, he lost his perspective. Then he went into God's house and thought on God's ways, and he adjusted his focus. The psalmist realized that no matter how successful the wicked seemed to be on earth, their destiny was eternal separation from God. And, in contrast, he knew God, and God knew him.

*Yet I am always with you;*
*you hold me by my right hand.*
*You guide me with your counsel,*
*and afterward you will take me into glory.*

*Whom have I in heaven but you?*
*And earth has nothing I desire besides you.*
*(Ps. 73:23–26)*

The psalmist had learned that when you have nothing left but God, you realize He is enough. Your questions will not all be answered. Your circumstances may not be improved. The person you set your heart on may not live up to your expectations, *but God is the strength of your heart and your portion forever.*

The prophet Habakkuk learned this same lesson. After God revealed to him that Babylon would conquer and destroy his country, Habakkuk came to the conclusion that no matter what his circumstances were, He would find his joy in God. His words could, and should, be ours.

*Though the fig tree does not bud*
*and there are no grapes on the vines,*
*though the olive crop fails*
*and the fields produce no food,*
*though there are no sheep in the pen*
*and no cattle in the stalls,*
*yet I will rejoice in the LORD.*
*I will be joyful in God my Savior. (Hab. 3:17–18)*

# 15

## Dwarfed by Discontentment

MY NEIGHBOR CLAUDINE'S FACE was always set in a mask of discontent. For years, I'd see her out my kitchen window as she would water her garden, carry in her groceries, or talk to her children, and I couldn't help but notice that a deep frown was a permanent fixture on her face. Her mouth was set in a long, hard line that rarely curved into a smile.

When I talked to Claudine over coffee, I quickly learned that nothing was ever good enough for her. Her house might be attractive, but it needed paint and her husband was too lazy to paint it. Her kids might be polite, good students, but they were too much like her in-laws to suit her taste. The weather might be nice, but if all this sunshine kept up, we'd soon be facing a drought.

Claudine was unable to enjoy anything fully because there always was a fly in the ointment. If she didn't see it immediately, she'd find it eventually. The poor woman was chronically dissatisfied. Her discontentment was like an ulcer that gnawed away at her sense of gratitude, her peace of mind, and her enjoyment of life.

## A Hindrance to Spiritual Growth

Discontentment is an emotion that is capable of dwarfing us spiritually because it is directed against the Lord. If we are discontented with His will for us, then we're not going to grow in our faith.

The people of Israel on their journey from Egypt to Canaan provide a rich source of illustrations for this particular emotion. We've already seen how their complaining affected their leader, Moses. They often discouraged him and angered him. As we move forward, we'll see how their discontentment affected their own lives and brought God's judgment upon them.

None of us will ever be able to imagine what it must have been like for at least two and a half million people who had been slaves for four hundred years to be set free from their bondage. For one thing, their freedom wasn't provided by a presidential emancipation paper. Their deliverance was a spectacular demonstration of the sovereignty and power of the Most High God who had chosen them to be His people.

God totally devastated Egypt, a proud nation that had ruthlessly oppressed the Hebrews. He humiliated the Pharaoh, who had arrogantly asked, "Who is the Lord that I should obey Him?"

Now the Israelites were gathered safely on the eastern shore of the Red Sea, which they had crossed on dry ground. Egypt lay in ruins behind them. "And when the Israelites saw the great power the LORD displayed against the Egyptians, the people feared the LORD and put their trust in him and in Moses his servant" (Exod. 14:31).

Take a few minutes to read Exodus 15—it is the song the people sang to celebrate God's victory. They sang and danced in joy and freedom. They were on a mountaintop, dizzy with the wonder of it all. If God could deliver them from Pharaoh, He could do anything!

But it didn't take long for their point of view to change. First came three days without water. Then they found a spring that only poured forth bitter water. Soon came the ominous words that stamped their character throughout their journey: "The people grumbled against Moses, saying, 'What are we to drink?'" (Exod. 15:24).

The principles God demonstrated to the discontented Israelites so long ago are still strategic to us as we seek contentment in today's world.

## Discontentment Comes When We Focus on What We Lack

The solution was so simple. The Lord had no intention of abandoning His people. He just wanted their trust. When Moses appealed to the Lord, He showed Moses what to do: "Then Moses cried out to the LORD and the LORD showed him a piece of wood. He threw it into the water, and the water became sweet" (Exod. 15:25).

Less than a month later, we find the people not only grumbling but looking back to Egypt with nostalgia. "In the desert the whole community grumbled against Moses and Aaron" (Exod. 16:2).

The food they had brought with them was gone. Already they had only a selective memory of their slavery in Egypt, recalling not their bondage but the meals provided by their masters. They whined, "There we sat around pots of meat and ate all the food we wanted." So they accused their leaders of wrong motives, saying, "You have brought us out into this desert to starve."

In response, Moses and Aaron put the right perspective on the Israelites' discontent. The two leaders told them, "Who are we, that you should grumble against us? . . . You are not grumbling against us, but against the LORD" (Exod. 16:7–8).

## Discontentment Is Directed Toward God

The Israelites were dissatisfied with God and the way He was handling things. Whenever they came to an obstacle that required faith in the Lord who led them, whether it was thirst or hunger, they complained. They could have encouraged each other by saying, "God has brought us this far; He must have a plan to take care of us the rest of the way." But they never did. Their immediate response was to question God's motives and to doubt His goodness and his power. They were never content to just rest in Him.

What about us? How do we react to difficulties? Do we angrily add them up as examples of the way God has let us down? Is the glass half-full or half-empty for us? Do we shake our fists at heaven and say, "Why did You let this happen to me?" Do we withdraw from God, refusing to read our Bibles or pray?

Or do we say, "Lord, You have cared for me so far, I trust You to supply the wisdom and the resources I need for this situation. I am content to leave it in Your hands." Our attitudes make all the difference in the way we face our circumstances.

## Need Teaches Us to Trust God More

Of course, as far as His people were concerned, God had a plan. And His plan was something they never could have even imagined. He knew they had to eat. He knew there were no supermarkets in the Sinai wilderness. He knew they couldn't plant gardens and wait for food to grow and still travel at the same time. So He just sent fast food— bread from heaven that contained all the nourishment they required. All they had to do was to go out every morning and pick it. The manna fell wherever they were every day.

But the Israelites never seemed to learn from these incidents. Their faith didn't grow with each demonstration of God's provision. They seemed determined to be discontent. Manna was not enough to satisfy them. For example . . .

"They camped at Rephidim, but there was no water for the people to drink. So they quarreled with Moses and said, 'Give us water to drink.'

"Moses replied, 'Why do you quarrel with me? Why do you put the LORD to the test?'

"But the people were thirsty for water there, and they grumbled against Moses. They said, 'Why did you bring us up out of Egypt to make us and our children and livestock die of thirst?'

"Then Moses cried out to the LORD, 'What am I to do with these people? They are almost ready to stone me'" (Exod. 17:1–3).

They continually quarreled and grumbled, and Egypt was looking better all the time. Of course, they had forgotten a few small items regarding Egypt: bondage, oppression, cruelty, and death. However, God was still patient with them. He satisfied their thirst by supplying a river of water from a rock.

## Discontentment Distorts the Past and Destroys the Present

Do you look back on the "good old days" of your life and think you were happier then than you are now? Stop and ask yourself whether you were really content back then. Wasn't there always something else you wanted to make you happy? Discontentment casts a dark shadow on our lives. It's a worm that nibbles away at our peace and joy.

Israel's dissatisfaction reached its zenith when God brought the people to Mount Sinai. He spoke in an audible voice that thundered from the mountain. Then he called Moses up to Him, and for forty days He gave Moses the Law His people were to live by and the plans for the tabernacle, where He would dwell among them. Unfortunately, forty days was too long for those chronically discontented people.

"When the people saw that Moses was so long in coming down from the mountain, they gathered around Aaron and said, 'Come, make us gods who will go before us. As for this fellow Moses who brought us up out of Egypt, we don't know what has happened to him'" (Exod. 32:1).

It's rather hard to believe, but the people weren't satisfied with what God had already done. And since their circumstances weren't exactly the way they wanted them to be, they decided to exchange God for a golden calf.

This time God was infuriated, and He punished many of them with death. But when Moses interceded for the people, God forgave them, and they continued on their journey. However, God's patience was finally wearing thin. Each time their discontent erupted, the punishment was more severe.

"Now the people complained about their hardships in the hearing of the LORD, and when he heard them his anger was aroused. Then fire from the LORD burned among them and consumed some of the outskirts of the camp. When the people cried out to Moses, he prayed to the LORD, and the fire died down.

"The rabble with them began to crave other food, and

again the Israelites started wailing and said, 'If only we had meat to eat! We remember the fish we ate in Egypt at no cost—also the cucumbers, melons, leeks, onions, and garlic. But now we have lost our appetite; we never see anything but this manna'" (Num. 11:1-2, 4-6).

First the Israelites complained about the hardships of their journey; God sent fire to consume some of them. Then they complained about the steady diet of manna; God sent them quail enough to eat for a month, and many of them died as they ate it. Then came the last straw—they refused to enter the wonderful land God was giving them as a gift. Ten of the twelve spies discouraged them from obeying God and taking possession of the land. They reported huge, dangerous inhabitants of the land who seemed to grow larger and more menacing with each telling of the story. They said, "We seemed like grasshoppers in our own eyes and we looked the same to them. . . .

"That night all the people of the community raised their voices and wept aloud. All the Israelites grumbled against Moses and Aaron, and the whole assembly said to them, 'If only we had died in Egypt! Or in this desert! Why is the Lord bringing us to this land only to let us fall by the sword? . . . We should choose a leader and go back to Egypt'" (Num. 13:33b and 14:1-4).

## Discontentment Results in Rebellion

After two years of seeing God miraculously meet their every need, the people were dissatisfied with His care and His purpose for their lives. Their hearts yearned for Egypt. Egypt was their homeland, not Canaan. They had blanked out the agony of slavery; they lusted for the food of Egypt. They were still slaves in their hearts—slaves to their cravings.

Their constant dissatisfaction and complaining led to rebellion. This time God was finished with them.

When Moses pled with God to forgive them the Lord responded, "I have forgiven them, as you asked. Nevertheless, as surely as I live and as surely as the glory of the LORD fills the whole earth, not one of the men who saw my glory and the miraculous signs I performed in Egypt and in the desert but who disobeyed me and tested me ten times—not one of them will ever see the land I promised on oath to their forefathers. No one who has treated me with contempt will ever see it" (Num. 14:20–23).

## Discontentment Prevents God from Giving Us His Best

It was all over for the discontented. They wandered in circles for thirty-eight more years like one long funeral procession as that generation lived their lives without anticipating anything but death. The people's dissatisfaction with God's purpose for them, their disdain of His bountiful provision, their disregard of His mighty power, and their distrust of His great love brought them to a point of no return. God had no more patience and provided no more second chances. It was all over. They were alive, but they looked at a bleak future that led nowhere but to the grave.

Why should we study this ancient story? Maybe you've already noticed that it bears a striking resemblance to our own emotional behavior. Discontent lurks in each person's heart. If it existed in Eden, it exists everywhere. That's why God tells us we need to carefully study Israel's experiences with God. As Paul wrote, "Now these things occurred as examples to keep us from setting our hearts on evil things as they did. Do not be idolaters, as some of them were; as it is written: 'The people sat down to eat and drink and got up to indulge in pagan revelry.' We should not commit sexual immorality, as some of them did—and in one day twenty-three thousand of them died. We should not test the LORD, as some of them did—and were killed by snakes. And do not grumble, as some of them did—and were killed by the destroying angel" (1 Cor. 10:6–10).

## Discontentment Is Sin

The temptation to sin usually begins with discontentment about what we are or what we have. For instance, consider financial sins. How much grief would be avoided if we were satisfied with our income? If we didn't crave more and more of the things money can buy, would we enslave ourselves to creditors? "Whoever loves money never has money enough; whoever loves wealth is never satisfied with his income" (Eccles. 5:10).

Another example of discontent involves emotional and sexual adultery. Immorality and the devastation it brings on families, individuals, and society would never happen if men and women were satisfied with their mates. As the wise Solomon wrote, "May you rejoice in the wife of your youth. . . . May her breasts satisfy you always, may you ever be captivated by her love" (Prov. 5:18–19).

Sinful actions always spring from ungodly thoughts and attitudes. An ungrateful, discontented spirit is an open door to unholy behavior, causing us to turn our backs on God and take matters into our own hands. This kind of rebellion doesn't have to happen. God is faithful, and we don't have to yield to the temptation to be discontented with our families, salaries, jobs, and life in general. Temptation is not a sin, but yielding to it is. What should be the attitude of a woman who is a child of God by faith in Jesus Christ and is indwelt by the Holy Spirit? We find the answer in Paul's letter to the Philippians:

"Do everything without complaining or arguing, so that you may become blameless and pure, children of God without fault in a crooked and depraved generation, in which you shine like stars in the universe as you hold out the word of life" (Phil. 2:14–16a).

"Do everything?" Does this mean the housework, the carpool, the visits to parents, church work, or community service? *Do everything without complaining?* Yes, that's what God's Word says.

Naturally, we don't develop this kind of positive attitude without some instruction. For example, I used to hate to fold clothes. With five children, there was always quite a lot of it. Then I heard someone say that while she folded clothes, she thanked God for each person in her family and prayed for him or her. What a difference that simple attitude adjustment made!

## You Can't Be Godly and Discontented

When I studied the word *content* as it is used in the New Testament, I found something very interesting. In other places the same Greek word is translated, "enough," "sufficient," and "to be strong enough." Obviously, godliness and contentment go together like hand and glove. And "godliness with contentment is great gain. For we brought nothing into the world, and we can take nothing out of it. But if we have food and clothing, we will be content with that" (1 Tim. 6:6–8).

The woman whose heart is filled with Jesus will be grateful for every blessing, and she will trust Him through every difficulty. We won't like to admit it, but we really can live with just the bare necessities—food, clothes, and shelter. In fact, in many parts of the world, people are relieved to have that and can't imagine having anything more. And we have so much more than just the essentials—we have a heavenly Father Who will not abandon us. He knows what we need, and He has promised to supply it. What He wants most from us is simple, childlike trust. But that's not always easy for us because it doesn't come naturally.

## Contentment Must Be Learned

The apostle Paul *learned* to be content. His physical circumstances did not determine his attitude or control his emotions. He wrote, "I am not saying this because I am in need, for I have learned to be content whatever the circumstances. I know what it is to be in need, and I know what it is to have plenty. I have learned the secret of being content in any and every situation, whether well fed or hungry, whether living in plenty or in want. I can do everything through him who gives me strength" (Phil. 4:11–13).

He said the secret to being content is knowing that Jesus Christ gives us the strength we need to do whatever He wants us to do. The secret of being content is believing that Jesus is sufficient.

In another familiar passage, Paul had a physical infirmity that he pleaded with God to remove: "Three times I pleaded with the Lord to take it away from me. But he said to me, 'My grace is sufficient for you, for my power is made perfect in weakness.' Therefore I will boast all the more gladly about my weaknesses, so that Christ's power may rest on me" (2 Cor. 12:8–9).

The Lord told Paul, "Don't be upset and discontented

because you are limited by this infirmity. My grace will make you strong enough to bear it. You'll have to depend on Me every day, and I'll be here. So you can be content because I will be enough for all your needs."

## We Can Be Content Because God's Resources Are Limitless

We are instructed to be more than grateful—God wants us to share our blessings with others. Paul wrote, "Each man should give what he has decided in his heart to give, not reluctantly or under compulsion, for God loves a cheerful giver. And God is able to make all grace abound to you, so that in all things at all times, having all that you need, you will abound in every good work" (2 Cor. 9:7–8).

The phrase "having all that you need" is represented by the same Greek word that is translated "content" in other places. Are you getting the picture? We don't have to greedily hang on to our possessions, fearful that we won't have enough for our own needs. We can give cheerfully and generously to the Lord, knowing He will see to it that we always have enough for ourselves and enough to give away.

## We Can Be Content Because God's Presence Is Constant

God's Word tells us to be content, satisfied with our material resources and physical condition because the Lord is with us: "Keep your lives free from the love of money and be content with what you have, because God has said, 'Never will I leave you; never will I forsake you'" (Heb. 13:5).

How can we possibly depend on health, money, and possessions for our security when we have the Lord, and He promises never to forget, neglect, nor abandon us? We are precious to Him. We are His children, and He is our perfect Father.

## Facing Frightening Possibilities

This lesson of trusting God became a part of my life in a way I will never forget when, after a breast examination, I had a call from the diagnostic center. There was something irregular about my mammogram, and the doctor wanted me to come in the next day for further tests. Maybe you know just how I felt. You can't help the thoughts that crowd your imagination. *Suppose it is cancer. Has it spread? Do I have to look ahead to surgery, chemotherapy, and death?*

During that time, I was studying the meaning of the Greek word used for "content," and it was a revelation to me in a new way. I'm always telling people to look at the worst-case scenario and then tell the Lord you trust Him no matter what. Now it was my turn.

I began to see that no matter what the additional tests might reveal, the Lord would be with me and He would be enough. He would be sufficient. He would make me strong, whatever the verdict was. Having Him is better than health, better than wealth, better than any form of security or happiness we depend on. And what is death for a child of God? It is nothing but a dark valley we walk through, our hand in His, as He ushers us into His glorious presence for all eternity.

I can't tell you the joy and peace all this gave me. When my children called and asked if I was worried, I said, "No. No matter what happens, the Lord is enough. I can't complain. I've had very good health for all these years. I'm not immune from any disease." That peace stayed with me all day, all through the further exams. Even when I waited in the examining room for the doctor, looking at the picture on the sonogram of this dark, alien thing in my breast, there was peace. Then the doctor came in, and I asked, "May I call my husband in?"

The doctor replied, "Well, all I want to tell you is that it's a benign cyst filled with fluid."

Of course, I was happy. But I know the day may come when the news will not be good. I only hope that I will still be satisfied and contented because I have the Lord and He is enough to meet my every need. His grace is sufficient. But it's only there when we need it. God's grace is not available to us when we envision the future, imagining trouble ahead of time.

## The Fear of the Lord Brings Peace

"The fear of the LORD leads to life: Then one rests content, untouched by trouble" (Prov. 19:23). *Fear of the Lord* means a loving reverence for God, and that includes submission to His Lordship and His Word.

Do you see how revering God, being content with your life and enjoying its blessings, and trusting Him through its difficulties will bring stability to your emotions? You won't be at the mercy of every new circumstance.

To be "untouched by trouble" doesn't mean we won't have troubles. This is a fallen world, and trouble and suffering are part of life here on earth. "Untouched by trouble" does mean trouble will never touch the inner core of our being where we live with God. Troubles will not devastate our faith—on the contrary, they will give us endurance and maturity. We can be content, even in our trials, because God is sufficient. Is discontentment your problem? If so, gratitude to God for His faithfulness is your solution.

# 16

~~∙∞∞∙~~

## The Agony of Grief

MY FRIEND ELIZABETH BECK was happily heading for the tennis courts one morning when she stopped by her husband's office to say hello. She was surprised when the receptionist told her there had been "a change in plans" and that she should go home instead. Puzzled, Elizabeth went home and found her husband, Rob, waiting for her in the kitchen. That's when her life changed forever. She has graciously agreed to share her story here:

Rob told me that our son, Michael, and his fiancée, Lori, had been killed when their car was hit by a drunk driver the day before—Mother's Day.

Mike and Lori lived in California; we were living in Charlotte, North Carolina. Rob had received a phone call from one of Michael's law professors, telling him of their deaths.

We were a very religious family. Michael had

accepted Christ in college, and he and Lori were both committed Christians. But when Michael had tried to explain to me his new relationship with Jesus Christ, I hadn't been able to understand what he meant.

Now we were in the agony of grief. We flew to California for the funerals, and a couple of months later we moved to Dallas. There, my days followed a strange routine. I would get our young daughter, Emily, off to school, then I would take a long shower. After I dressed, I would go to the grocery store, buy a small bag of candy, walk home, and eat it all.

I repeated this routine several times a day. There was a big hole under my diaphragm, and I tried to fill it by eating something sweet or spicy.

At the end of eighteen months, I was in the shower one day—actually on my hands and knees—and I called out to Christ, "I don't know what all this means. I don't know what being born again means. I don't know what it means to give my life to You. But whatever it means, You can have my whole life. You're going to have to take it because I can't go on this way. Whatever it is You want from me, You have it."

Instantly, everything was different. I found myself standing upright again. The pain was still there, but the despair was gone. Amazingly, as I dressed, the phone rang, and a casual friend said, "The Lord has laid it on my heart to ask you to go to Bible Study Fellowship. Would you be interested?"

I said, "Yes, what is it?" I knew I had to go.

I was able to start a few days later. I bought a Bible, went to classes, struggled with the questions. There were wonderful women in my discussion group, women who loved me and prayed for me.

The weekend before Easter, my nephew invited me to the Easter program in his church because he would be playing his violin. I went and was in a very emotional state through the whole program. When the crucifixion was portrayed, I was crying. I thought, *Christ died for Michael.* And then, very clearly in my mind I heard, *Elizabeth, I died for YOU!*

I had always known that Christ had died for mankind. Now, for the first time, it was *personal.* Now my spiritual growth really took off. I thirsted for God's Word. I understood the great truths of the Bible at last. I started to go to church, and I got involved in the women's ministries and met wonderful new friends.

In addition to this, Rob and I wanted to do what we could to prevent what had happened to us from happening to others. We got involved with Mothers Against Drunk Driving (MADD); Rob eventually became chairman of its board of directors.

I was determined that the victims of drunk drivers be more than statistics; I wanted them to be seen as persons with names. So I spoke in many places, naming Michael and Lori and showing their pictures. I now look back at the worst incident in our lives and realize that our grief brought us into a personal relationship with our Lord Jesus Christ. Our faith in Him enabled us to make a difference in the lives of others who faced grief.

Elizabeth's story reminds us again of how painful grief can be—and how powerfully God uses every part of our lives, good and bad, to bring us into a closer relationship with Him. Did the Becks' grief automatically end when they found a new purpose in their lives? No, of course not. They would miss their son for the rest of their lives. But now they had hope and a sense of peace that God was with them, even in the midst of their pain. And there was one more step in their healing. Elizabeth continues:

> The Lord made it possible for me to do something that for me was impossible. I had struggled for a long time with bitterness against the man who had killed our son. Even though I knew I should forgive him, I absolutely couldn't do it.
>
> Finally a friend suggested that I forgive the man *through Christ*. I made a mental picture of the man with a transparency of the picture of Christ placed over it so that I could see the man's picture only through Christ's image. I depended on the Lord to enable me to forgive.
>
> Some time later, a friend commented, "It's wonderful to see that you're over your bitterness and hatred for the man who killed Michael."
>
> I hadn't even realized it, but the Lord had answered my prayer.

## Loss Brings Pain; Pain Brings Grief

Probably one of the hardest things we have to face is loss. For parents like the Becks, it's the loss of a child. We also lose parents and friends to death. We lose mates through death or divorce. We lose health and have to adjust to an entirely different lifestyle. We lose the companionship of friends because someone moves. We lose jobs. Engagements are broken. Friendships are betrayed. These losses cause us to sorrow and to grieve, deeply affecting our emotions.

Grief is a feeling of deep mental anguish caused by loss. It can be the loss of a loved one, loss of possessions, loss of a career, or some other life-changing loss. Grief can also be sorrow for something that someone has done or failed to do.

Because we live in a fallen world, life inevitably includes sorrow. When sin entered the human race, it brought death—physical death and spiritual death with all the accompanying ramifications. Death or loss of anything we value causes grief. However, God has a higher purpose for His people, and He is faithful to use our most painful times to mature us, to draw us into closer dependence on Him.

## One Grieving Woman

A woman in the Old Testament suffered the loss of everything. She was no stoic, no super saint. She felt the bitterness and hopelessness that accompanies grief. As we study Naomi, we will learn a lot about the God who cares for us in our grief.

Here's how Naomi's story unfolded: Because there was a famine in Israel, a Hebrew man named Elimelech took his wife, Naomi, and his two sons, Mahlon and Kilion, to live in a neighboring country called Moab. The family only intended to stay temporarily, but once they settled down in that godless society, they remained there for ten years. In that time the two sons married pagan women.

During those Moab years, I'm sure Naomi, in particular, felt a sense of loss. They were aliens, away from family and friends, and now she had two Moabites for daughters-in-law.

She must have thought, "If only we had stayed in Bethlehem. I'd have daughters-in-law from my own people who understand our faith and customs." But the worst was yet to come:

"Now Elimelech, Naomi's husband, died, and she was left with her two sons. . . . After they had lived there about ten years, both Mahlon and Kilion also died, and Naomi was left without her two sons and her husband" (Ruth 1:3–5).

Naomi's future could not have been more hopeless, because she had no one to provide for her. In Israel, if a widow had no family she was cared for by the community. But they didn't have such humane laws in Moab. So when the news came that the famine had ended in Israel, she prepared to go back home. When she told her two daughters-in-law what she intended to do, they wanted to go with her. But she said, "Return home, my daughters. Why would you come with me? Am I going to have any more sons, who could become your husbands?" (Ruth 1:11).

## Take Time to Feel Your Pain

It's clear that these women loved each other. They had all suffered terrible losses, and they wept together at the thought of separation. They demonstrate something important: God gave us tears to express our grief. As the beautiful passage from Ecclesiastes reminds us, "There is . . . a time to weep and a time to laugh, a time to mourn and a time to dance" (Eccles. 3:1, 4).

Here is a primary lesson: If you are experiencing grief for any reason, allow yourself time to mourn and weep. If you try to hold in your tears and to ignore your pain, there may be serious problems later. God gave us tears to shed in our grief, an outpouring of our inner pain.

One of the most freeing verses in the Bible is also the shortest one. When Jesus came to the home of Mary and Martha after Lazarus had died, He saw their grief. Even though He knew that in just a few minutes He would raise Lazarus from the dead, the Scripture simply says, "Jesus wept" (John 11:38).

Those two words give us permission to weep in our sorrow because they reveal how Jesus modeled for us this normal response to grief. Don't think it's more spiritual to hold in your tears.

Naomi wasn't afraid to feel her grief. Not only was she in extreme pain, but it is quite clear who she blamed for her loss. "'The LORD's hand has gone out against me! . . . Don't call me Naomi,' she told them. 'Call me Mara, because the Almighty has made my life very bitter. I went away full, but the LORD has brought me back empty. Why call me Naomi? The LORD has afflicted me; the Almighty has brought misfortune upon me'" (Ruth 1:13b, 20–21).

I would say Naomi was pretty depressed, wouldn't you? "The Lord's hand has gone out against me. He has afflicted me, emptied me, brought misfortune on me, made my life very bitter."

Her misery was evident in her demeanor, because once she got back to Israel, her old friends hardly recognized her. She still had no certainty about the future. By now, her daughter-in-law Ruth had insisted on returning to Bethlehem with her, but how were they to live? Naomi felt abandoned by God, and she had no reason at this point to think otherwise.

We can learn some valuable principles about grief from Naomi and her amazing story. Throughout the rest of this chapter, we'll study these principles and learn godly ways to deal not only with our own grief but with the grief of others.

## Grief May Cause Despair or Depression

During times of sorrow, our emotions are like a roller coaster. On the downside, we shouldn't be surprised by feelings of despair or depression—those feelings don't mean we're unspiritual. In her despair, I'm sure Naomi asked the questions we all ask when sorrow comes. *Why? Why did God allow this? Couldn't He have stopped it? Couldn't He have saved my job? Why did my husband have to die so young? Couldn't He have healed my child? Couldn't God have restored my marriage?*

I heard a few months ago that one of my friends in New York was killed instantly in a bizarre accident. She was driving home from seeing her mother in a nursing home when a landscaping truck pulling a trailer crossed three lanes and the median and hit her head-on. My friend was a gentle, gracious, caring woman with a loving husband, children, and grandchildren. I found myself thinking, *If only she had been one car length ahead or behind. Why did God let that happen?*

The Old Testament saints did not believe in second causes. They believed in God's sovereignty over the world and the people in it. When Elijah held the dead son of the widow he stayed with during the famine, he cried out to God, "O LORD my God, have you brought tragedy also upon this widow I am staying with, by causing her son to die?" (1 Kings 17:20).

When Job heard the news that he had lost everything, he said, "The LORD gave and the LORD has taken away; may the name of the LORD be praised" (Job 1:21).

God can handle it when we question His ways and put the blame on Him. But He wants us to accept what He sends us and still trust His goodness and His love. He has a purpose for our sorrow and loss.

## Believe That God Will Use Your Sorrows for Your Good

Some of our afflictions come as consequences of sin, and others are intended to keep us from sin. Some come to make us draw closer to God and to enable us to grow spiritually. Some heartaches simply make us realize that God's way is best. Whatever the pain, God means it for good in our lives just as he did in Joseph's. It's worth repeating what Joseph was able to say twenty years after he lost everything through the hatred and cruelty of his brothers: "You intended to harm me, but God intended it for good to accomplish what is now being done, the saving of many lives" (Gen. 50:20).

Joseph certainly couldn't have said those words the first thirteen years of his life in Egypt, but he saw God's purpose clearly seven years later. Sometimes it may take years for us to see the pattern God had in mind when He brought sorrow into our lives. But we do know this: God is sovereign. Nothing happens in heaven or earth that He does not know about and even permit. That is tough theology. But if we don't believe it we will swing aimlessly over an abyss of unbelief, uncertainty, and despair.

Think of the worst loss you have ever suffered, and consider these important questions:

- Can you think of anything good that's come out of it?

- Did it draw you closer to God?

- Have you seen answers to prayer because of it?

- Have you been able to help others just because of what you've experienced yourself?

- Do you have more compassion for others?

God uses everything in our lives to make us more like

Jesus. And Jesus was a "man of sorrows and acquainted with grief" (Isa. 53:3 NKJV). How can we bypass sorrow and grief and still expect to develop emotional and spiritual maturity? We just can't decide to skip that course!

Even though Naomi didn't see it, God had a plan to meet her need and restore her faith and joy. He used her hopeless situation to get her back to the land where He could bless her. And best of all, He gave her Ruth, a daughter-in-law who was committed to her for life.

### Ruth—Naomi's Great Blessing

Naomi and Ruth returned to Bethlehem at the beginning of harvest time. There was no welfare system in those days, but there was a way for the poor to get help. Farmers could only reap their fields once. Grapes could only be picked from the vines once. The widows and the poor were then to glean what was left over. This was workfare, not welfare. And since Ruth was the younger and stronger, she spoke up: "'Let me go to the fields and pick up the leftover grain behind anyone in whose eyes I find favor.'

"Naomi said to her, 'Go ahead, my daughter.' So she went out and began to glean in the fields behind the harvesters. As it turned out, she found herself working in a field belonging to Boaz, who was from the clan of Elimelech" (Ruth 2:2–3).

"She found herself working in a field belonging to Boaz." Ten little words. But behind them is the hand of Almighty God keeping His promise to defend "the cause of the fatherless and the widow, . . . giving [them] food and clothing" (Deut. 10:18).

### God Is Working Even Though We Can't See It

God's plan for Ruth and Naomi was not an endless struggle for existence. He had a wonderful future planned out for them, but He didn't reveal it to them ahead of time. It would be nice if God would tell us His plans before they come to pass. But what He really wants from us is faith— simple, childlike trust in His goodness, power, and love.

When Naomi heard whose field Ruth had gleaned in, she responded enthusiastically.

"'The LORD bless him!' Naomi said to her daughter-in-law. 'He has not stopped showing his kindness to the living and to the dead.' She added, 'That man is our close relative; he is one of our kinsman-redeemers'" (Ruth 2:20).

Boaz was a close relative of Elimelech's. The law in Israel stated that when a man died childless, his brother or closest relative was to marry the widow and have a child by her. That child would belong to the dead man and inherit his property. When Boaz stepped into her life, Naomi's faith was given a shot in the arm. God had not abandoned them; He had arranged things so Ruth would end up in Boaz's fields. And Boaz treated her with kindness and generosity.

## Look Forward to the Future with Hope

When Naomi returned to Bethlehem, she arrived in a hopeless state of mind. That is often one of the results of grief. When we grieve, we can see nothing but a bleak and empty future. But if we keep remembering that God loves us and has the power to help us and provide for our future, we are able to keep hope alive and our faith will remain strong.

The rest of the book of Ruth is a wonderful romance. Boaz loved Ruth, and Naomi instructed Ruth in the way to claim her rights under the covenant. Boaz immediately and gladly did all the legal things necessary to make Ruth his wife.

"So Boaz took Ruth and she became his wife. Then he went to her, and the LORD enabled her to conceive, and she gave birth to a son. . . .

"Then Naomi took the child, laid him in her lap and cared for him. The women living there said, 'Naomi has a son.' And they named him Obed. He was the father of Jesse, the father of David" (Ruth 4:13, 16).

Ruth had been barren all the years she was married to Mahlon. Now the Lord gave her a son, and Naomi had a family again. Naomi's old age was secure. God had not abandoned her. In fact, He had arranged all the details to fill her emptiness, provide for her needs, and restore her faith and her joy. This little grandson didn't carry a drop of Naomi's blood, but he was hers! And though she didn't live to see it, Obed became the ancestor of King David and ultimately of the Lord Jesus Christ. In Matthew 1:5, Boaz and Ruth are specifically mentioned in the genealogy of the Savior.

What Naomi and Ruth enjoyed in their happy ending was much more than they had lost, even though they couldn't comprehend the full dimensions of the compassion and blessings of God.

## Jesus Showed Us That God Has Feelings

Jesus came, in part, to reveal to us what the invisible God is like. What Jesus felt, God still feels. Listen to the Lord's description of Himself to Moses in Exodus 34:6: "The LORD, the LORD, the compassionate and gracious God, slow to anger, abounding in love and faithfulness, maintaining love to thousands, and forgiving wickedness, rebellion and sin."

Compassion, anger, and love are all emotions. God feels, so He knows how we feel when we suffer loss. As the psalmist wrote, "But you, O God, do see trouble and grief; you consider it to take it in hand. The victim commits himself to you" (Ps. 10:14).

# The Agony of Grief

During Jesus' ministry, He came upon a funeral procession. The dead person was the only son of a widow, and she was accompanied by a large crowd of mourners, who shared her grief. In Luke 7:13, we read of Jesus' reaction to this tragic scene: "When the Lord saw her, his heart went out to her and he said, 'Don't cry.'"

Then Jesus touched the coffin, "and those carrying it stood still. He said, 'Young man, I say to you get up!' The dead man sat up and began to talk, and Jesus gave him back to his mother."

Can't you see Jesus gently saying to this grieving mother, "Don't cry"? Then He simply brought her son back to life. The response to this wonderful miracle demonstrated to the people that God was a God of compassion. The people "were all filled with awe and praised God. 'A great prophet has appeared among us,' they said. 'God has come to help his people'" (Luke 7:16).

The widow's loss and the ensuing miracle were used by God to validate the claims of Jesus that He is the Son of God. God will still use our grief to bring glory and praise to Himself if we keep on trusting Him.

## Avoid Emotional Extremes

When we are hurting, there are two extremes to avoid. One extreme is to block our emotions, determined that we will never care so much that we can be hurt that way again. It is unhealthy to block our emotions to protect ourselves. God wants us to feel so we are able to taste life in its fullness. The other extreme is becoming so consumed by our grief that nothing else matters. The best thing to do is to get back into the normal process of life again. I so admire women I know who've been widowed and continue to live fruitful, unselfish lives. They are involved with other people, helping and serving wherever they can.

## Comforting Those Who Grieve

Those who have suffered loss know better than anyone else some important principles for comfort. Let's consider a few of those guidelines for encouraging the grieving:

### Be Available for the Long Run

Everyone is there in the midst of the crisis, but after the funeral is over and the visitors are gone—that's the time to check up on the grieving person. Be there just to talk. Go with her to help handle legal details if she needs it. Suggest doing things with her to help get through this period of sorrow. If you and your husband have been friends with the couple, don't leave the widow out of social invitations now that she's alone.

### Be Sensitive and Flexible in Your Communication

Don't assume that the grieving woman doesn't want to talk about her loved one. You may be tempted to say, "Let's not talk about it; it'll only make you feel bad." Many times, it's a comfort to talk about the person we've lost. It keeps the memory real. It helps to know someone else valued our lost loved one, too.

If you're visiting those who are dying, don't pretend they are going to get well. Give them a chance to talk about their death if they want to. Remind them about heaven, and assure them you will meet them there. Since the Lord Jesus

Christ proved His victory over death by His resurrection, death for the believer is the entrance to eternal glory. There will be normal grief, but we shouldn't sorrow as those do who have no hope.

## Don't Use Pat Phrases to Comfort Others

It's hard to know what to say to someone who is grieving. It may be easier to remember what not to say. For example, avoid saying, "I know how you feel." One young mother whose child had died at birth was told, "I know just how you feel. My cat died last week."

Don't say, "Time is a great healer." Don't even quote Romans 8:28 when the wound is raw. Tell the grieving person you are praying for her or him. Say something like this: "I can only try to imagine what you must be feeling. But I want you to know that I love you and I am available to do anything you want me to."

Don't say, "Call me if I can do anything." That puts the burden on the grieving person. Instead, you take the initiative. Offer to run an errand, pick up relatives at the airport, clean the bathroom, or answer the phone.

## Trust God to Be the Comforter

We must recognize our limitations and remember that God is the one who "heals the brokenhearted and binds up their wounds" (Ps. 147:3). We should do all we can do to ease others' pain, but we can't do what only God can do. He is "the God of all comfort, who comforts us in all our troubles" with a comfort that is transferable.[1] In a fallen world where loss and grief are guaranteed, God will use us to comfort others when wounds are raw and deep.

As women of God, we have authenticity because we

ourselves have come through the valley of sorrow and tears, and our faith remains stronger than ever. God is real. The promises of Scripture are true. There is life after loss. The future is as bright as the promises of God. And time is not even the size of a period on this page when compared to eternity. All separation is temporary for believers. One day we will be forever with the Lord and with each other.

In the book of Revelation, God offers one final word about our grief: "Then I saw a new heaven and a new earth, for the first heaven and the first earth had passed away. . . . And I heard a loud voice from the throne saying, 'Now the dwelling of God is with men, and he will live with them. They will be his people, and God himself will be with them and be their God. He will wipe every tear from their eyes. There will be no more death or mourning or crying or pain, for the old order of things has passed away'" (Rev. 21:1a, 3–4).

# 17

## Lessons in Loneliness

KATE ROLLED OVER at the sound of the alarm, glanced at the clock, and wondered if she wanted to get up. Why bother? The house was silent. All three of her children had left for college over the past two days, and their absence hung heavily in the air. To make matters worse, the family dog had died a month ago, and even his friendly little wagging form had been removed from her life.

She wandered into the kitchen where her husband Hank was reading the sports page. "Hi, honey," she murmured.

"Hmmm . . ."

Hank's eyes never left the paper. She poured herself a cup of coffee and sat down at the window, staring at the September garden.

Hank stretched and groaned, got up and headed for the closet. Grabbing his suit coat, he walked toward the front door. "See you . . ." The door slammed, and Kate listened as the car started and backed out of the driveway, its sound fading into the cool morning air.

How would she fill another empty day? Kate dialed a couple of friends' phone numbers, but reached only their answering machines. She turned on the TV, made her way around the channels, then flipped it off in frustration. "I'll go to the mall," she decided aloud, smiling grimly at the bumper-sticker reality: "When the going gets tough, the tough go shopping."

The mall was crowded. Kate was caught in a tide of last-minute back-to-school shoppers, yet the crowds made her feel lonelier than ever. She sat at Starbuck's sipping a latte, watching the people chattering, laughing, and smiling at each other. Tears stung her eyes—she felt like the oldest shopper in the mall and the only one shopping alone. She fought off the idea that the world had somehow passed her by.

When she got home, Kate began to look forward to Hank's return from work. She decided to fight off her depression by making his favorite meal, which she did. The sound of his car pulling into the driveway gave her a surge of hope. Her solitary confinement was over!

Unfortunately, although Hank seemed to enjoy the dinner, he did so without comment. "How was your day, honey?" she inquired sweetly.

"Fine. Where's the *TV Guide?*"

She handed it to him, and he studied it during dessert. While she cleaned up the kitchen, Hank turned on the first in the series of sitcoms he would watch for the next three hours. Kate had a choice. She could sit at his side and watch with him. Or she could go into the den and spend the evening reading the new book she'd bought during her mall excursion. Either way, she would find no relief from the loneliness that seemed to follow her everywhere, dogging her steps like an unwelcome companion.

## Lonely, But Not Alone

*Loneliness.* Even the word sounds sad, doesn't it?

What does it mean? Is being with people a solution? Is being married a remedy? Is having lots of friends a sure cure? Is being alone the same as being lonely?

According to Les Carter, "Loneliness is a *feeling* of separation, isolation, or distance in human relations. Loneliness implies emotional pain, an empty feeling, and a yearning to feel understood and accepted by someone."[1]

Here's another interesting observation from Tim Hansel: "Loneliness is not the same as being alone. Loneliness is feeling alone . . . no matter how many people are around you. It is a feeling of being disconnected, unplugged, left out, isolated."[2]

This means that we can be in a crowded room and feel isolated, locked in a bubble of our own. Like Kate, we can be married and lonely, yearning to be accepted as we are. This is one of the saddest kinds of loneliness there is. We can be at family gatherings and feel at a distance from other relatives. Loneliness is a feeling, not a circumstance. And all of us have felt it at some time because I don't think it's possible to find anyone who feels completely understood and fully satisfied all the time.

## A Man Called to Loneliness

As we consider loneliness, we're going to revisit a man we met a few chapters ago. God called the prophet Jeremiah to live a very lonely life, and his loneliness came as a result of his commitment and obedience to God. In fact, that might be the very reason why some of us feel isolated and distanced from members of our families and some of our friends today.

As we read in Jeremiah 1 and 2, God called Jeremiah to be a prophet, a spokesman for God. He was to give God's words to a nation of idolatrous, wicked people. His messages were to be warnings of impending disaster, a judgment upon their rebellion against God and their worship of the pagan idols around them. We know Jeremiah was not courageous by nature; in fact he was timid and insecure. But God promised to make him strong and able to stand alone against the whole nation.

It was clear from the beginning that Jeremiah would never be a popular preacher who told people nice things about themselves. His message didn't exactly build their self-esteem. He gave them God's Word—and they hated it! Nobody ordered tapes of his messages. He didn't make many friends. Instead, he made very powerful enemies. To make matters worse, the Lord gave Jeremiah some very hard orders. We find them in chapter 15 of the book of Jeremiah:

"Then the word of the LORD came to me: 'You must not marry and have sons or daughters in this place.' For this is what the LORD says. . . . 'They will die of deadly diseases. They will not be mourned or buried but will be like refuse on the ground.' . . . 'Do not enter a house where there is a funeral meal; do not go to mourn or show sympathy, because I have withdrawn my blessing, my love and my pity from this people.' . . .

"'And do not enter a house where there is feasting and sit down to eat and drink. . . . Before your eyes and in your days I will bring an end to the sounds of joy and gladness and to the voices of bride and bridegroom in this place'" (Jer. 16:1–5, 8–9).

Jeremiah would never know the intimacy, comfort, and joys of marriage and family. He couldn't even enjoy a normal social life, sharing the joys and sorrows of his community. God wanted his lonely life to be an object lesson for what would soon happen to the whole nation. Talk about isolation and loneliness! There was no safe place, humanly speaking, for Jeremiah to be loved, encouraged, and accepted.

God gave His prophet a very tough assignment, and it lasted more than forty years, growing progressively worse. It's a real comfort to me to observe that Jeremiah wasn't always on top of things. He had deep feelings. There were times when he mourned for his people and times when he bitterly complained about his lot in life, including his relationship with God. Here are just a few of his grievances:

"Since my people are crushed, I am crushed; I mourn, and horror grips me. Is there no balm in Gilead? Is there no physician there? Why then is there no healing for the wound of my people? Oh, that my head were a spring of water and my eyes a fountain of tears! I would weep day and night for the slain of my people" (Jer. 8:21–9:1).

"Alas, my mother, that you gave me birth, a man with whom the whole land strives and contends! I have neither lent nor borrowed, yet everyone curses me! . . .

"I am ridiculed all day long; everyone mocks me. Whenever I speak, I cry out proclaiming violence and destruction. So the word of the LORD has brought me insult and reproach all day long" (Jer. 15:10 and 20:7–8).

Wouldn't you agree that Jeremiah was a very lonely man? He was angry, frustrated, fearful, uncertain, and depressed. He knew his enemies wanted to get rid of him. He couldn't trust his friends. He felt sometimes that even

God had deceived him. His life was so painful he wished he had never been born.

The interesting thing is that he expressed his feelings. He told God what he was thinking. Some of his complaints were a mixture of good and bad. He'd complain, then he'd remember God's promises, then he'd complain again. The reason Jeremiah was able to fulfill his mission for all those years was that he always came back to the Lord and remembered his promises to him. He said, "Ah, Sovereign LORD, you have made the heavens and the earth by your great power and outstretched arm. Nothing is too hard for you" (Jer. 32:17).

In the same way that Jeremiah was distressed because he believed God's promises of disaster and exile, he was encouraged and enabled to endure because he believed God's promises of a future restoration of Israel to the land that would be permanent. In the generations to follow, there would be no rebellion because God would bring His people under a new covenant that would be written on their hearts, not on tables of stone (see Jer. 31:31–34).

## The Strength to Go On

Jeremiah could bear the hatred, the treachery, the plots against him, the imprisonment, the loneliness, even being stuck in the mud in the bottom of a cistern till he almost starved to death—he endured it all for the Lord's sake. He endured it because he knew he was doing what God told him to do, and he could see the big picture. He believed God would bring His people back to the land and to Himself. And even though Jeremiah wouldn't live to see it, he found comfort in its certainty.

Some of us experience isolation and distance from husbands, mothers, fathers, sisters, and brothers, just because we are believers and are living in obedience to God. Perhaps you aren't invited to family gatherings. Maybe your husband is angry because you won't do some of the things he wants to do. Or it could be that some of your friends have dropped you since you've begun to be serious about living according to Scripture. Jesus knew this would happen to those who trusted Him. He invited us to take an eternal perspective on what happens to us here for His sake, saying, "Blessed are you when people insult you, persecute you and falsely say all kinds of evil against you because of me. Rejoice and be glad, because great is your reward in heaven, for in the same way they persecuted the prophets who were before you" (Matt. 5:11–12).

Just as Jeremiah demonstrated for his people what was in their future, Jesus modeled for us what we can expect when we choose the narrow road of faith and obedience.

Imagine growing up with Jesus as a big brother—He must have been easy to live with, because He never sinned at all. Yet in spite of that fact, when he embarked on His ministry, His own brothers didn't believe in Him and thought He was crazy (see John 7:5 and Mark 3:21). He often felt isolation and lack of intimacy with His disciples in the three years He was training them. They were selfish, ambitious, unspiritual, and often unbelieving. Even when He needed them most as He prayed in the garden before His agony, they kept falling asleep, unable or unwilling to share that terrifying, heartbreaking time with Him.

Jesus certainly knew what it was to have His closest friends betray, deny, disappoint, and abandon Him. And the worst part about His substitutionary death for us was enduring, in the hours He hung on the cross, a seeming eternity of separation from God—the penalty for sin.

There was ultimate loneliness in Jesus' heart-rending cry: "My God, my God, why have you forsaken me?" (Matt. 27:45). He endured separation from God, which is spiritual death, so we would never have to know it. He died to spare us the agony He experienced. And He lives today, willing to help us solve the problem of our lonely feelings.

## The Causes of Loneliness

There are three basic causes for feelings of loneliness or alienation: separation from God, from others, and from ourselves. Let's examine each of these causes and consider ways to ease the pain of loneliness.

### Separation from God

God created us to live in fellowship with Him, but sin broke that fellowship. As human beings, we are born with a capacity to know God; but we are also born without the knowledge of God and without a relationship with Him. God loved His fallen race so much that He sent His Son, the Lord Jesus, to die for our sins so that we might be restored to fellowship with God through faith in Christ.

Even those of us who have trusted Him and have been given new life experience times when we feel alienated from our heavenly Father. Fortunately, we're always the ones who have moved away—sin breaks our fellowship with God. That's why He has provided a way for us to be continually cleansed and forgiven when we confess our sins to Him. He doesn't want us to be lonely for Him.

We may be lonely for people, for friends, for a mate, but

if we have trusted the Lord Jesus Christ, we never have to be lonely for God again. We have His constant assurance that He is always with us and in us. Augustine rightly said, "Our hearts are restless, O God, until they find their rest in Thee." In order to grow closer to Him, we need to cultivate our fellowship with God. There are some practical ways we can do that:

*Quiet Time.* Take just fifteen minutes at the start of your day to read some Scripture and pray.

*Memorize Scripture.* During the day, when you have to wait in a doctor's office or even at a traffic light, work on memorizing a verse you have in your purse or taped to your dashboard. Have verses available in your office desk so you can work on them at lunch or during your breaks. You'll be surprised at how many lost minutes you can recapture in a day.

*Practice the Presence of God.* Send up "arrow prayers" all day. Keep the spiritual "phone lines" open. This will cause you to be more responsive to the nudging of His Spirit. You will be more sensitive to sin. You will be more obedient to His Word. And you'll find that your close fellowship with your heavenly Father will ease the loneliness, which is the worst of all, that sense of separation from God.

## Separation from People

God also created us to have relationships with other people. When He first created Adam, He said, "It is not good for man to be alone." But every relationship has its times of stress and disappointment. We all want to be perfectly free to be ourselves and to be accepted as we are, but that never works 100 percent of the time. There are times, for various reasons, when close friendships are disturbed.

Occasionally, we even feel a distance from those we love the most.

It's very lonely to know a lot of people who are just acquaintances. We all put on happy faces when we meet. But how do we establish the kind of friendships in which we can be ourselves? How do we connect at a meaningful level? There are some steps we can take.

*Reach Out to Others.* Instead of waiting for the phone to ring, take the initiative. Many times the friend you want to know better is waiting for someone to call her. Suggest lunch or a casual dinner at your place. Plan an outing together, if you are both interested and compatible.

*Share a Common Interest or Service.* Another way to make friends is within church groups. Women get better acquainted when they share studies or serve in an outreach together. As we work side by side, share our needs, and pray together, we find other women who are drawn to us, and vice versa. Women need each other. We accomplish more as a team than we could ever accomplish alone.

*Accept Others As They Are.* Don't make friends to reform them. This doesn't mean that friends can't help each other overcome bad attitudes and flaws. But it can't be done within the context of condemnation. Love is the great motivator. When I know that I am loved and appreciated, it's not as painful to hear someone advise me that I should try a different approach to a situation.

*Share Your Thoughts As Your Confidence Grows.* Friendships deepen when we realize we can trust another person. Once trust is established, we are able to open our hearts to each other, drop our masks, and be real. Many times we struggle with loneliness because we keep our problems and real feelings all bottled up inside. But when we begin to talk about them, they are whittled down to size. Even if a friend has no solution, just talking about a difficulty helps. Knowing that someone else cares and is praying for us often eases our sense of isolation. We need to recognize that pride is often what keeps us from being honest and real, adding to our sense of isolation.

Sometimes our feelings of loneliness indicate a sense of alienation from ourselves. When we are completely honest, we'll admit there are things in our personalities we don't like. There are times when everything seems to be going wrong and we are frustrated and discouraged. When we dwell on our failures and shortcomings, we generate our own loneliness. And this usually leads to more problems.

There are some positive efforts we can make to change our sense of self-alienation:

***Respond to God's Love.*** Choose to believe that God loves you, and receive His love. You are His unique creation. He will give your life significance. When you and I accept God's evaluation of us, we won't be controlled by our own feelings of inadequacy and loneliness. We will have confidence in His ability to make us the person He wants us to be. We will be free to be ourselves, controlled by His Holy Spirit. When you know you are loved, it changes the way you feel about yourself.

Jeremiah's isolation and loneliness were eased when he remembered who God is and when he believed His promises. Jesus experienced the worst separation in time and eternity so that we could have the love, fellowship, presence, and guidance of God forever. The psalmist said it well:

*Yet I am always with you;*
*  you hold me by my right hand.*
*You guide me with your counsel,*
*  and afterward you will take me into glory.*
*Whom have I in heaven but you?*

*  And earth has nothing I desire besides you.*
*My flesh and my heart may fail,*
*  but God is the strength of my heart*
*  and my portion forever. . . .*

*As for me, it is good to be near God.*
*  I have made the Sovereign LORD my refuge;*
*  I will tell of all your deeds. (Ps. 73:23–26, 28)*

The psalmist's words are as true today as they were then. We may be alone, but we don't have to be lonely all the time.

Knowing God loves us and has control of our lives should give us an assurance that He will meet our needs. He may not give us all we want, but He will give us what we need. If you have been living with a feeling of loneliness and you've put your life on hold until things change, stop it today! Tell the Lord that knowing Him is more important than any other relationship. Tell Him you want to get out of the spiritual playpen and grow to maturity. Emotional immaturity will hinder your spiritual maturity. Your feelings aren't the most important part of you.

***Act with Your Will.*** God gave you a will so you can make choices, and He intends for you to act with your will. He wants you . . .

- To choose to obey Him.

- To choose to be satisfied with the life He's given you.

- To choose to be thankful for the way He has made you.

- To choose to accept the love, forgiveness, peace, joy, and fellowship He offers you in the Lord Jesus Christ.

Every blessing of God is wrapped up in Jesus. When we act with our will to receive Him for our salvation, He comes to live within us, bringing with Him all the promises of God. We don't have to look anywhere else to find joy, peace, acceptance, security, and significance. We must simply act with our wills to receive whatever we need from Him. Provision for our every need is offered to us without cost, through the mercy and grace of God. But it isn't really ours until we take it for ourselves—by faith.

# 18

≈∘≈

# Friendship's
# Precious Gift

**W**HEN JENNY ARRIVED HOME from work, she was exhausted and on the verge of tears. Her boss, who was normally unreasonable and impatient, had been nothing short of a madman all day long. He had yelled, cursed, and blamed her for everything that had gone wrong in his life for the last six months. Of course he would apologize tomorrow, as usual, but today had taken its toll.

Just as she walked through the door the phone rang. *If it's him, I'm hanging up!* she promised herself. But instead of her boss's angry roar, she was relieved to hear the calm voice of her friend and neighbor Sara. "Why don't you come over for dinner? I made enough lasagna for an army!"

Jenny left her suit and high heels in a heap on the floor and pulled on her jeans and a sweatshirt. She quickly walked across the greenbelt to Sara's condo, which was filled with plants, books, candles, and friendly clutter. "I already fed the kids," Sara laughed. "They're at the pool, so we can talk in peace. How was your day?"

Jenny shook her head. "It doesn't get much worse than today. Have you got any Tylenol?"

Sara frowned as she shook two pills out of an ample bottle and handed them over. "So when are you going to quit? That boss of yours is such a jerk—you could probably sue him for some kind of abuse."

"I've sent my resumé to three different headhunters— they're supposed to be scheduling interviews starting next week. Meanwhile, I just need to keep my mouth shut. Thank goodness tomorrow's Friday!"

Before long, the conversation had shifted from Jenny's problems to Sara's mother's health, and then on to other concerns the two women shared. Before Jenny left, Sara prayed with her, asking the Lord to protect her and to give her a better job. By the time Jenny got home, her troubled feelings had diminished.

Just before ten o'clock the phone rang—it was a friend of Sara's, telling her about a job opportunity that might be coming up at her office. "Don't worry," the woman encouraged Jenny. "The Lord will lead you to something, even if this idea doesn't work out. I'm just sorry you're having such a hard time."

In spite of everything, Jenny slept serenely that night. The heavy pressure of stress had been lifted from her chest, and her last waking thought was a prayer of thanksgiving. "Lord, I'm so grateful for friends like Sara. Please bless her for being there when I need her . . ."

## The Value of Friendship

In the preceding chapters we've considered some painful emotions that can profoundly hinder our spiritual growth: Fear, anger, grief, loneliness, and many more. So why conclude the book with a lesson on friendship? It's true that friendship isn't really an emotion. But it has a lot to do with our emotions because it is vital to our emotional and spiritual maturity.

Friendships affirm our worth, and they whittle away at our self-centeredness. In healthy friendship there is giving and receiving. There is affection, commitment, concern, interest, loyalty, and love. To maintain healthy friendships we have to pay a price.

A woman who doesn't have at least one close friend suffers a loneliness that increasingly corrodes her sense of worth and drives her into isolation. Friendlessness can make us suspicious of others' motives. It prevents us from revealing ourselves, so that we perpetuate the very thing that causes us so much pain. A lack of at least one close friend can seriously impede our spiritual growth, because God has designed us to be members of a body. And every part needs the other parts to grow healthy and strong.

Women particularly need and long for friendships with other women. Dee Brestin, in her book *The Joy of Women's Friendships,* makes an interesting point when she says, "The role of the mother has an enormous impact on the ability of a child to love. . . . Many sociologists speculate that one of the main cultural reasons that the friendships of women tend to be warmer, stronger, and more plentiful than the friendships of men is due to the mother/daughter relationship. In America, and in many countries, the primary caretaker in early childhood is the mother. Therefore, little girls have experienced a deep same-sex friendship in their formative years—whereas many little boys have not. For women, being close to another woman feels very natural. For men being close to another man may feel quite unnatural. This may explain, in part, why most women yearn for a same-sex friendship in their adult years, whereas most men are content to have their only close friend be a woman."[1]

Someone has said that, "Friendship creates the world in which we can comfortably be ourselves, in which we are valued above all for that." Don't we all long for friends who love us for ourselves, just the way we are?

## An Ancient Model for Friendship

Ironically, the ideal friendship about which Scripture gives us many details is not between two women, but between two men, Jonathan and David. Let's trace their friendship and discover some truths that will help us to be better friends to one another. We can learn some specific principles about our own friendships as we examine theirs.

Jonathan's father, Saul, was king of Israel, and Jonathan was heir to the throne. The people of a neighboring nation, the Philistines, were sending raiding parties into Israel, and Saul had an army in the field to defend his country. Jonathan was one of his generals. Saul's strategy was to take a defensive posture, but Jonathan's was to attack. Jonathan was a man of action. At one point, Jonathan and his armor-bearer won a battle for the entire nation (see 1 Sam. 14:6–15, 20, 22–23).

Eventually, the Philistines tried a different approach. They sent out a champion, a giant of a man, who challenged the armies of Israel to send out one of their men to fight him. The army of the winner would be the victor. Every morning and evening for forty days, Goliath had been shouting his challenge to the terrified army of Israel.

"On hearing the Philistine's words, Saul and all the Israelites were dismayed and terrified" (1 Sam. 17:11).

Saul, who should have inspired his men's courage, was shaking like a leaf along with his men. Then a young shepherd boy showed up. David had been sent by his father to the camp to see how his brothers were faring. When he heard Goliath's challenge, he was outraged. Everyone knows the story of Goliath's demise, brought about by young David's slingshot. (If you'd like to read it again, it's in 1 Samuel 17.) The story of David's victory over Goliath helps us understand an important aspect of David's friendship with Jonathan: They had a lot in common.

## True Friends Have Something in Common

After David's heroic encounter with Goliath, it's easy to see why David and Jonathan became such inseparable friends.

- They both took the initiative to act.

- They both had great faith in God's power.

- They both had courage despite the odds against them.
- They both experienced God's deliverance in battle.

- They both inspired loyalty in others.

- They both were men of integrity.

- They both led others to victory.

- They both were loved by the people. (see 1 Sam. 14:45; 18:16.)

- They were men who thought and acted alike.

That's why Jonathan opened his heart in a commitment

to David that lasted all his life. And that brings us to another important aspect of friendship . . .

## True Friends Are One in Spirit

"Jonathan became one in spirit with David, and he loved him as himself. From that day Saul kept David with him and did not let him return to his father's house. And Jonathan made a covenant with David because he loved him as himself. Jonathan took off the robe he was wearing and gave it to David, along with his tunic, and even his sword, his bow and his belt" (1 Sam. 18:1–4).

Jonathan believed something Saul refused to accept. Samuel the prophet had already told Saul that God had rejected him as king. Because of his disobedience, God had chosen a man after His own heart to be king after Saul. The throne would not be handed down to Saul's son.

When Saul's son Jonathan gave David his robe, tunic, sword, bow, and belt, he was acknowledging the shepherd boy David as his peer. But more than that, I believe Jonathan knew this was the man God had chosen to be Israel's king, even though Samuel had anointed David in a private ceremony, and it was unlikely anyone outside David's family knew about it.

Jonathan was, in effect, stepping aside. There was no jealousy in his heart, no attempt at keeping his distance, no desire to protect his privileged position.

Did you ever meet someone and hit it off immediately? If so, you probably made the effort to see each other again and developed a friendship. Do you have a friend now who sees eye to eye with you on most important things? Are you alike in your responses? Although opposites attract and add diversity to our lives, there's a freedom to relax, explore, and grow in a friendship where there is oneness in spirit.

## True Friends Love Each Other Selflessly

Twice we read that Jonathan loved David as himself. Actually, Jonathan loved David *more* than himself. He willingly gave up any hopes that he would succeed his father, and he entered into a covenant friendship with David. From then on he was concerned with David's interests over his own. And in this relationship, Jonathan had more to give than David did.

Do you have a friend for whom you will sacrifice your time, plans, and resources when she needs you? Have you stopped in the middle of a busy day to rush to her side in an emergency? Do you pray for her and with her? Do you call to keep in touch daily when she's going through a difficult experience? Do you invite her for meals? Do you plan an outing that will interest and divert her? Do you care for her children so that she and her husband can get away for a night?

When we love someone else as much as we love ourselves, it means we will sacrifice ourselves for them. We'll be there when they need us.

Saul was delighted with David's military prowess and put him in charge of the military campaigns against the Philistines. The people loved him too. But Saul's pleasure turned into fear and jealousy as David's popularity increased. Saul gradually realized that this young man could most definitely replace him. So he tried to kill David a couple of times and plotted his death in many other ways. Nothing worked. David came out of every situation alive and well.

## True Friends Protect and Intercede for Each Other

As Saul became more and more mentally unstable, he did something that put Jonathan in a very tough spot. Jonathan was forced to choose between loyalty to his father, who was doing wrong, and his friend David.

"Saul told his son Jonathan and all the attendants to kill David. But Jonathan was very fond of David and warned him, 'My father Saul is looking for a chance to kill you. Be on your guard tomorrow morning; go into hiding and stay there. I will go out and stand with my father in the field where you are. I'll speak to him about you and will tell you what I find out'" (1 Sam. 19:1–3).

At this point, Jonathan tried to convince his father Saul that he shouldn't kill David, who had done him no wrong. He reminded him that David had been used by God against Goliath. Somehow, at least for the time being, he changed his father's mind. "Saul listened to Jonathan and took this oath: 'As surely as the LORD lives, David will not be put to death'" (1 Sam. 19:6).

## True Friends Are Honest with Each Other

What do you do when someone says something unkind or untrue about a friend of yours? Do you believe it? Do you speak up? Do you try to reconcile them? Or do you say nothing. Remember: Evil prospers when good people remain silent. A true friend protects her (or his) friends. As wise King Solomon said, "A friend loves at all times" (Prov. 17:17).

Sadly, in David's story, it wasn't long before Saul made two more attempts to kill David. This time the younger man fled for his life. He first went to Samuel, the prophet, to tell him all that had happened. But then he turned to Jonathan.

"Then David fled from Naioth at Ramah and went to Jonathan and asked, 'What have I done? What is my crime? How have I wronged your father, that he is trying to take my life?'" (1 Sam. 20:1).

## True Friends Are There in Times of Trouble

By this time, David was more realistic about Saul than Jonathan was. Jonathan thought he had his father's confidence. He thought he could continue to protect David. But Saul's spear had been thrown at David twice, so David knew how murderous Saul really was. David was afraid, and he was able to say so to Jonathan. He didn't pretend, posture, or put on a brave front. He freely expressed his feelings and fears to his friend.

Do you have a friend like that? Are you that kind of a friend yourself? Can your friends be honest with you about their feelings? Do you empathize? Do you weep with them? Or are you quick to pat them on the back, say something spiritual, preach a little sermon, and go on about your business? True friendship provides a safe place to honestly express yourself and still be loved.

Jonathan looked at his distraught friend and made his decision. He told David, "Whatever you want me to do, I'll do for you" (1 Sam. 20:4).

## True Friends Want God's Will for Each Other

David suggested a plan that would reveal Saul's true intentions toward him: "Tomorrow is the New Moon festival, and I am supposed to dine with the king; but let me go and hide in the field until the evening of the day after tomorrow. If your father misses me at all, tell him, 'David earnestly asked my permission to hurry to Bethlehem, his hometown, because an annual sacrifice is being made there for his whole clan.' If he says, 'Very well,' then your servant is safe. But if he loses his temper, you can be sure that he is determined to harm me" (1 Sam. 20:5b–7).

In response to David's words, Jonathan made a covenant with David that would extend to his descendants.

"By the LORD, the God of Israel, I will surely sound out my father by this time the day after tomorrow! If he is favorably disposed toward you, will I not send you word and let you know? But if my father is inclined to harm you, may the LORD deal with me, be it ever so severely, if I do not let you know and send you away safely. May the LORD be with you as he has been with my father. But show me unfailing kindness like that of the LORD as long as I live, so that I may not be killed, and do not ever cut off your kindness from my family—not even when the LORD has cut off every one of David's enemies from the face of the earth" (1 Sam. 20:12–15).

In those days, when a new dynasty took the throne, often the members of the preceding royal family were killed so that there wouldn't be any rivals stirring up rebellion. Jonathan knew David would be king and that he would not be. He asked for his own life and that of his family.

Jonathan had all the qualities necessary to be a good king. He was not disqualified because of his own failure but because of his father's. He could have been bitter and resentful because his future power and glory were lost to him. But Jonathan embraced God's will for himself and for David, his friend.

## True Friends Do Not Compete with Each Other

How do you feel when a friend succeeds in something you felt you were qualified for? Did you have a friend who was chosen as cheerleader in high school and you didn't make the squad? Were you as close after that? What happens to a relationship when an old friend moves to an expensive new house and you are still struggling to survive in your starter home? Or has a baby when you've been trying for years to get pregnant?

Jealousy and envy are like termites that eat away at the structure of a friendship, leaving nothing but sawdust. God has given each of us unique abilities. When we accept God's will for ourselves and our friends, we will not be in competition with them but will genuinely rejoice in their success. We will show them, as Jonathan said, "unfailing kindness."

In Hebrew, the original language of the Old Testament, Jonathan used a wonderful word for unfailing kindness. *Hesed* describes the Lord's unconditional, unfailing, loyal love and faithfulness to His people. Jonathan said, "unfailing kindness like that of the Lord."

## True Friends Are Loyal to the End

Jonathan was not reluctant to demand of David a guarantee that extended to his descendants. He loved David and trusted his integrity to keep this covenant he asked of him. Do your friends know you are loyal to them? Can they trust you to be faithful to them? Can they trust you to extend your love to their children? Do you have a friend you feel that way about?

I have a friend who makes an effort to see my children and maintain a relationship with them. I can't tell you how much I appreciate her love for them. One friend like that will bless us for a lifetime!

## True Friends Grieve When Separated

In this case, Jonathan tested his father, and Saul failed

the test. So Jonathan met David at the place they planned.

"David got up from the south side of the stone, and bowed down before Jonathan three times, with his face to the ground. They kissed each other and wept together—but David wept the most.

"Jonathan said to David, 'Go in peace, for we have sworn friendship with each other in the name of the LORD, saying 'The LORD is witness between you and me, and between your descendants and my descendants forever.' Then David left, and Jonathan went back to the town" (1 Sam. 20:41–42).

They wept in genuine grief because they would no longer be able to be together openly. Their fellowship was over; their friendship could only be enjoyed secretly and at a distance. David became a fugitive from the king's murderous jealousy. He was on the run for ten years. From then on, Saul's major military campaign was against David. "Day after day Saul searched for him, but God did not give David into his hands" (Sam. 23:14b).

Before I left Long Island and moved to Texas, there were two women I was especially close to. We laughed at the same things. We could say anything we felt to each other and be understood. After I moved away from them, I remember feeling so lonely for them.

There's something special about friends who knew you when you were young. You had similar struggles in the early years of marriage. Your children grew up together. There are memories that can't be duplicated in later years. Someone has said, "New friends are like silver, but old friends are like gold." Keep in touch with old friends even when there's distance between you. The memories are too good to forget.

## True Friends Build Each Other Up Spiritually

Scripture tells us of only one more meeting between these two dear friends. "While David was at Horesh in the Desert of Ziph, he learned that Saul had come out to take his life. And Saul's son Jonathan went to David at Horesh and helped him find strength in God. 'Don't be afraid,' he said. 'My father Saul will not lay a hand on you. You will be king over Israel, and I will be second to you. Even my father Saul knows this.' The two of them made a covenant before the LORD. Then Jonathan went home, but David remained at Horesh" (1 Sam. 23:15–18).

Jonathan helped David find his strength in God. He encouraged his faith. Jonathan couldn't be with David, but God was with him every moment. Jonathan believed David would be king, and he was willing to take second place. What a big-hearted man he was! They renewed the covenant they had made before, and they parted for the last time.

Do your friendships have a spiritual dimension? We help each other most when we encourage each other to depend on God. When we remind each other of God's promises, it strengthens faith that may have wavered.

Do you pray for a friend who is in such pain she can't even pray for herself? For a believer, friendships cannot omit the life of the Spirit. They go far below the surface. This may mean sharing your faith in Christ with a friend who does not know Him. But it definitely means that in friendships between believers, Jesus Christ is included. It's a threesome.

Jonathan's hope that he would live to see David become king would not come true. In a final battle with the Philistines Saul and three of his sons were killed. One of these sons was Jonathan. When the news came to David, his grief was overwhelming. He wrote a lament recorded in 2 Samuel 1. He ended it with these words that spoke of his love for Jonathan:

> How the mighty have fallen in battle!
>    Jonathan lies slain on your heights.
> I grieve for you, Jonathan, my brother;
>    you were very dear to me.
> Your love for me was wonderful,
>    more wonderful than that of women. (2 Sam. 1:25–26)

"More wonderful than the love of women." These two men were second selves to each other—soul mates. It infuriates me to hear homosexuals insist that this means David and Jonathan had a homosexual relationship. This argument implies that two people can't have a same-sex friendship without the physical act of sex, which is patently ridiculous. As a matter of fact, the words used to describe the love Jonathan and David had for each other are never used in the Bible to describe a homosexual relationship. The word used for that is one that means to "know carnally" (Gen. 19:5).

## True Friends Keep Their Promises

What about the covenant David and Jonathan made and renewed about Jonathan's family? Years later, David remembered and kept his promise.

"David asked, 'Is there anyone still left of the house of Saul to whom I can show kindness for Jonathan's sake?'" (2 Sam. 9:1).

Jonathan had a son, Mephibosheth, who was five years old when his father died. A nurse, fleeing with him to save his life, had dropped him, and he was crippled for life. Now Mephibosheth had a son of his own. David sent for Mephibosheth.

"When Mephibosheth son of Jonathan, the son of Saul, came to David, he bowed down to pay him honor.

"David said, 'Mephibosheth!'

"'Your servant,' he replied.

"'Don't be afraid,' David said to him, 'for I will surely show you kindness for the sake of your father Jonathan. I will restore to you all the land that belonged to your grandfather Saul, and you will always eat at my table'" (2 Sam. 9:6–7).

David restored Mephibosheth's inheritance and adopted him into his own family for Jonathan's sake. Death did not end David's love for Jonathan. He faithfully kept the covenant he had made with him.

Can your friends trust you to be true to your word? Do you say you will call or visit, then fail to follow through? Are you full of excuses? Friendships must be nurtured and kept alive. They are too precious to neglect.

If you are longing for friendship, ask God to give you another woman who will be your friend. And commit yourself to being the kind of person she will want for a friend. Your emotional and spiritual growth won't really reach maturity if you are not able to be a friend.

## Friendship with God through the Lord Jesus

There's one more thing we should notice before we leave David and Jonathan. The loving-kindness David showered on Mephibosheth for Jonathan's sake is a picture of God's loving-kindness to us for Jesus' sake. Mephibosheth did nothing to deserve it. He was poor, helpless, and hopeless, afraid for his life. Likewise, we can do nothing to deserve God's loving-kindness to us.

Each of us was born a sinner, helpless and hopeless to change ourselves. Jesus' death and resurrection so satisfied the holiness and justice of God, that He can make us His children and give us an inheritance for Jesus' sake.

I hope you aren't trying to earn God's love. We cannot earn what He offers as a free gift. We must simply reach out and take the Lord Jesus Christ as our Savior. That's what it means to believe on Him. And that's how we are able to enjoy friendship with God, and therefore to share genuine, spiritual friendship with one another.

## Epilogue: A
## Final Word

God's purpose is for His children to keep on growing spiritually all their lives here on earth. He never intended that we stay in the crib and playpen. He wants each of us to be mature spiritually and emotionally. But we can't mature spiritually if we don't mature emotionally.

We've seen from God's Word how even the giants of the faith struggled with their emotions. How good it is of God to let us see beyond the surface, into the hearts and minds of men and women like Abraham, Lot, Jacob, Rachel, Leah, Joseph, Moses, Naomi, Ruth, David, Jeremiah, and Paul.

These folks were just like us. They suffered the hardships, difficulties, and tragedies of life in a fallen world. They struggled, they failed, they cried out to God, sometimes in confusion and doubt, always for help. And God came through for them. He forgave them, healed them, and used them to have an eternal impact on their contemporaries as well as on God's people throughout the many centuries since.

### "To Will and to Act . . ."

God hasn't changed. He has the same awesome power today He had then. He is a loving Father who wants His children to grow to maturity. He has given us all we need to do so: His Word to guide us, immediate access to Him in prayer, and the family of believers for fellowship and accountability. What he asks of us is obedience. But even there, He doesn't leave us to struggle on our own. He gives us His Holy Spirit to make us want to do His will and enable us to do it. "It is God who works in you to *will* and to *act* according to his good purpose" (Phil. 2:13 emphasis mine).

As we act with our wills to obey, regardless of our surging emotions, God is delighted with our faith and obedience. He will bring our emotions into line. He can and will deliver us, but we have to choose what we will believe. Will we keep believing what our capricious feelings tell us? Or will we believe what God tells us in His Word and act with our wills to obey Him? When we trust Him, He is free to exert all of His infinite power to help, to heal, and to deliver us. He will use our emotions in the process that transforms us and grows us up to maturity, conformed to the image of Jesus Christ, our Lord.

# Notes

### Chapter 1 ～∞～ Nurturing our Spiritual and Emotional Growth

1. Erwin Lutzer, *Managing Your Emotions* (Chappaqua, N.Y.: Christian Herald Books, 1981), 17.

2. I'm grateful to Erwin Lutzer for some of the insights that follow, which I found in his book *Managing Your Emotions*, published in 1981 by Christian Herald Books.

3. Lutzer, *Managing Your Emotions*, 11.

### Chapter 5 ～∞～ Nothing to Fear But Fear

1. 1 Cor. 6:18.

2. Amy Carmichael, "Thou Art My Lord Who Slept Upon a Pillow," from *Edges of His Ways*, copyright 1955, Dohnavur Fellowship, London. Used by permission of the Dohnavur Fellowship, England, and the Christian Literature Crusade, Fort Washington, Pennsylvania.

## Chapter 6 ~∞~ Weary of Worry

1. Frank Minirth, Paul Meier, and Don Hawkins, *Worry-Free Living* (Nashville: Thomas Nelson, 1989), 107–21.

2. Ibid.

## Chapter 7 ~∞~ A Disease Called Unforgiveness

1. Susan Forward, *Toxic Parents* (New York: Bantam, 1989), 189.

## Chapter 8 ~∞~ The Truth about Anger

1. Les Carter, *Good 'n' Angry* (Grand Rapids: Baker, 1985), 35.

2. This discussion of New Testament words describing anger is adapted from Richard Walters, *Anger* (Grand Rapids: Zondervan, 1981), 28ff.

3. Ibid., 29.

4. Carter, *Good 'n' Angry*, 14–16.

## Chapter 9 ~∞~ Envy—The Green-Eyed Tyrant

1. *The American Heritage Dictionary* (Boston: Houghton Mifflin, 1991).

2. Les Carter, *Mind Over Emotions* (Grand Rapids, Mich.: Baker, 1985), 52ff.

3. Ibid.

## Chapter 12 ~∞~ Pride's Subtle Masks

1. Luke 12:48 NKJV.

2. See James 4:6 and 1 Peter 5:5.

3. See James 2:1–9.

4. Carter, *Mind Over Emotions*, 145.

## Chapter 13 ∽∞∼ Inferiority—Another Form of Pride?

1. J. B. Phillips, *Letters to the Young Churches* (New York: McMillan, 1956), 74.

## Chapter 14 ∽∞∼ Dealing with Disappointment

1. I'm grateful to Dr. Paris Reidhead for sharing with me in a conversation several years ago this idea of a wedge-shaped progression of harmful emotions.

## Chapter 16 ∽∞∼ The Agony of Grief

1. See 2 Cor. 1:3–4.

## Chapter 17 ∽∞∼ Lessons in Loneliness

1. Carter, *Mind Over Emotions*, 121.

2. Tim Hansel, *Through the Wilderness of Loneliness* (Elgin, Ill.: David C. Cook, 1991), 59–60.

## Chapter 18 ∽∞∼ Friendship's Precious Gift

1. Dee Brestin, *The Joy of Women's Friendships* (Wheaton, Ill.: Victor/SF Publications, 1993), 10.

~~~~~~

# For Further Thought . . .

I HOPE THE IDEAS I've shared in this book have prompted you to consider how healthy, God-given emotions can enrich your life spiritually as well as in your everyday activities and attitudes.

To help you delve deeper into the lessons and suggestions presented in these pages, you might use these questions for personal or group study. They were designed to be studied ahead of the lesson. You'll find that your personal interaction with the Scriptures will give you a greater knowledge of the ways emotions can affect your life and enhance your relationship with God, with others, and with yourself.

## Chapter 1 ~ Nurturing Our Spiritual and Emotional Growth

1. *Read 1 Timothy 6:17.* Why did God give us emotions? What does this tell us about God in light of Genesis 1:26?

2. *Read John 1:12-13.* What is one of the wonderful things that happens when a person trusts Jesus Christ as his or her Savior?

3. Do you think of emotions in a positive or a negative way? Do you think there is a connection between your emotions and your spiritual life?

4. Are you controlled by emotions that hinder your spiritual growth, such as bitterness, envy, inferiority, or rejection? *Read Colossians 3:13-15* and write down a specific way you can begin to deal with an emotion that is a problem for you.

5. *Read Colossians 2:6-7 and Ephesians 4:11-13.* What is God's goal for his children?

6. *Read 1 Peter 2:2.* What is the first thing that is essential for growth to spiritual and emotional maturity? How does this help us mature?

7. *Read John 16:23-24 and Philippians 4:6-7.* What else is necessary for growth? Why is prayer needed if God is all-knowing? How does it help us mature?

8. *Read Hebrews 10:25 and Colossians 3:16.* Name something else that is necessary for growth to maturity. What benefits do we derive from being with other believers? Can you think of someone who has helped you mature?

9. *Read Matthew 7:24-27 and James 1:22-25.* Are studying Scripture, prayer, and fellowship with other Christians enough? What else is essential for our growth to maturity? Can you think of a time when you obeyed a specific Scripture and it changed your life?

10. *Read Hebrews 5:13-14.* How can disobedience retard your growth to maturity?

## Chapter 2 ∞ God, Our Healer

1. *Read Exodus 15:22-27.* What did God intend the healing of the bitter waters to teach His people? In what way was

this a test? What is usually your response to difficult circumstances? Can you think of ways God has tested you?

2. How did God reveal Himself here? What did the Israelites' future well-being depend upon? How would obedience to God's commands contribute to mental, emotional, and spiritual health for anyone?

3. *Read Isaiah 30:25, 57:17-18, and Psalm 147:3.* Whom and when does God promise to heal? *Read Isaiah 35:3-6* and write down what Isaiah said the Messiah would do when He came. *Read Acts 10:38* and record how Jesus fulfilled this prophecy.

4. *Read 2 Timothy 3:16-17.* Why can we trust God's Word? What will it do for us? Can you think of a specific time when God's Word rebuked, corrected, or instructed you in the right way to live?

5. *Read Isaiah 53:5.* Do you think Isaiah's statement, "by his wounds we are healed" refers only to physical healing? Is it a guarantee that we will always be healed when we ask for it? *Read 1 Peter 2:24* and see how Peter applies Isaiah's prophecy to Jesus. List some things for which we all need healing. Now write down one problem in your life for which you need healing. Note some Scripture verses that have encouraged you to turn to God for healing.

6. Scan one Gospel and note the different persons and conditions Jesus healed. Write down some of the words Jesus said to heal them. *Read Luke 7:1-10* and note what was remarkable about this incident. What was the only thing the centurion asked Jesus to do? *Read Psalm 107:1-2, 17-22* and find what God used to heal "those he redeemed."

## Chapter 3 ∾ Serving the Self

1. *Read Genesis 13:1-18, 19:1-38.* What did Abraham's

solution to resolve the quarreling among the herdsmen reveal about him? *Read Genesis 12:6-7.* What does Lot's choice reveal about him? What should Lot have remembered?

2. *Read Genesis 13:12-13, 14:12, and 19:1.* Trace Lot's assimilation into Sodom's society. What did his selfish choice cost him? What principle do you see here for us?

3. *Read Mark 9:33–37 and Luke 9:44–48.* What was one thing that motivated the disciples to follow Jesus? What were their expectations? How did Jesus define greatness? What example did He use? What characteristics of children did He want them to have?

4. *Read Matthew 20:17–28 and Mark 10:32–45.* What were the ambitions of James, John, and their mother? What was remarkable about the timing of their request? How did Jesus define greatness? Whom did He use as the example of greatness?

5. From the examples of Lot and the disciples, what do we learn about the effects of selfish ambition and self-centeredness on our character and our relationships?

6. *Read Galatians 5:19-20 and James 3:13–16.* What are the sources of self-centeredness and selfish ambition? What do these attitudes produce?

7. *Read Galatians 5:22-23; 1 Corinthians 13:5; Philippians 2:1-11; and Romans 12:10, 13.* What is the source of an unselfish interest in others? How will this be demonstrated in our interpersonal relationships? In our service for the Lord?

8. Is self-centeredness keeping you from spiritual maturity? Is there a particular area where this is obvious? Memorize a verse that helps you, and then apply it to your life.

## Chapter 4 ∼∞∼ The Burden of Guilt

1. *Read Luke 19:1–9*. Describe Zaccheus and his reputation. What was remarkable about what Jesus said to him? *Read Matthew 9:12-13 and Romans 5:8*. What does this tell us about Jesus?

2. How do we know that Zaccheus felt guilty? What did he confess? What did his intent to make restitution indicate? *Read Exodus 22:1, 3–4*. What must a person recognize before he or she trusts Christ as his or her Savior?

3. Why did Jesus say, "Salvation has come to this house"? *Read 1 Peter 3:18, Ephesians 1:7, and Hebrews 9:14*. Does just confession of sin and restitution save us? How does Jesus cleanse us of a guilty conscience?

4. *Read 2 Samuel 11 and 12*. What sins did David commit? Do you think he had a guilty conscience? *Read Psalm 32:3–4*. How long did he ignore it? Do you think he thought his cover-up had worked?

5. What does 2 Samuel 11:27 tell us? Why do you think Nathan approached David the way he did? Why was David so angry against the hypothetical man?

6. What was David's response to Nathan's statement, "You are the man"? *Read 2 Samuel 12:13 and Psalm 51*. How do we know David realized the enormity of his sin? Did God forgive him? Did he escape the consequences of his sins?

7. *Read 2 Samuel 12:14*. Why is it so serious when a believer flagrantly sins? *Read 1 John 1:9*. How can we be forgiven? On what basis does God forgive us? What does it mean "to confess our sins," and why is it necessary?

8. Do you feel guilty about something that is so bad you think God can't forgive you? What have you learned about God's forgiveness? Will you do what is necessary to receive it?

## Chapter 5 ~∞~ Nothing to Fear But Fear

1. *Read Genesis 27.* Why did Jacob leave home? What reasons did he have to fear Esau? Was Esau justified in his anger?

2. *Read Genesis 28:10–21.* What assurance did God give him on his journey? How did Jacob respond?

3. *Read Genesis 31:3, 11–13.* Why did Jacob decide to leave his father-in-law Laban after twenty years? *Read Genesis 32:1–2.* How did God continue to encourage him?

4. *Read Genesis 32 and 33.* With what attitude did Jacob approach Esau? Why was he so afraid? Analyze his prayer in Genesis 32:9–12. Do you ever pray like that? What did he expect to accomplish by his lavish gifts?

5. *Read Genesis 32:22–32.* What was the significance of Jacob's encounter with God? What should he have learned? What did he do next that proved he was still afraid of Esau?

6. Why do you think Esau's feelings about Jacob had changed? Did Jacob completely lose his fear of Esau? *Read Genesis 33:12–17.* What more could God have done to reassure Jacob?

7. Is there something you are afraid of? How does God give us confidence today to overcome our fears? *Read Psalm 34* every day for a week and write down what God promises to do for you. Choose one verse to memorize and pray it back to God every time you feel afraid.

## Chapter 6 ~∞~ Weary of Worry

1. *Read 2 Kings 6:8–23.* What did Elisha do repeatedly to frustrate the king of Aram's strategy? How did Elisha know his plans?

2. What did the king do to get rid of Elisha? Did the servant have a legitimate reason to be afraid? Where did he turn for help?

3. How did Elisha reassure the servant? What did the servant see? Did what the servant worried about ever happen?

4. What do we learn for ourselves from this incident? *Read 2 Corinthians 10:3–5, Ephesians 6:10–18, and Hebrews 1:14.* What provision has God made for our protection today? How should our awareness of God's promises affect our attitudes when we are involved in worrisome circumstances or relationships?

5. *Read Matthew 6:25–34.* List the reasons Jesus tells us not to worry. What command and promise does He give us in Matthew 6:33? Do you need to make an adjustment in your priorities to heed this command? How does this promise work as an antidote for worry?

6. What specific things do you worry about—health, marriage, children, money, abilities, social acceptance, friends, Christian life, the future? Write down your specific worries and apply to each item on your list the reasons Jesus gives not to worry. Then, with an act of your will, tell God you trust Him for each worry specifically. What will you do the next time that worry sneaks into your thoughts?

## Chapter 7 ~∞~ A Disease Called Unforgiveness

1. *Read Genesis 37.* Describe how Joseph's brothers felt about him. Why did they feel this way? Did Joseph deserve this hatred?

2. What does the brothers' treatment of Joseph reveal about their characters? What did it reveal about their feelings toward their father?

3. *Read Genesis 39–41*. Describe Joseph's character. Did his brothers' rejection and cruelty toward Joseph affect his integrity? Did false accusations or abandonment disillusion him? *Read Genesis 39:2–6, 21–23*. What was the reason for Joseph's success?

4. *Read Genesis 39:9; 40:8; and 41:16, 25, 28, 32, 38)* What was Joseph's view of God during the thirteen years of his bondage? What is remarkable about this in view of his circumstances?

5. Have you ever been unjustly treated or slandered? How do you feel about it? Have you become bitter? Have you withdrawn so you won't be hurt again? Have you become cynical about trusting people? Are you angry at God?

6. *Read Genesis 42–45*. Why do you think Joseph put his brothers through so much before he revealed himself to them? What did he want to be certain of? How had they changed?

7. What conclusions about the events of his life had Joseph come to during his long exile in Egypt? *Read Genesis 45:4–8 and 50:19–21*. Why was Joseph able to forgive his brothers?

8. How do you think the story might be different if Joseph had allowed bitterness and resentment to fester in his spirit? Are you bitter about something that has happened to you? Will you, by an act of your will, believe that God will use that difficult circumstance for good in your life and the lives of others?

### Chapter 8 ～∞～ The Truth about Anger

1. *Read Matthew 23, Mark 10:13–16, and John 2:13–16*. What made Jesus angry? What do we learn about God from this? What makes you angry? How do we distinguish

between anger that is sin and anger that is not sin?

2. *Read Exodus 32.* Whose anger does Exodus 32 describe? After reading this chapter, do you think anger is always a sin? Why or why not? What do we learn about God's anger in Exodus 34:6 and Psalm 30:5?

3. *Read Numbers 20.* What did Moses do from anger and frustration? Consider Moses' angry action in light of James 1:19-20. Can you think of an incident in your life where you spoke or acted rashly in anger? What was the result?

4. *Read Ephesians 4:26–27.* What is the warning in these verses? What is the practical advice on how to handle anger? What does it mean to "give the devil a foothold"? What might be some of the results?

5. *Read Galatians 5:19–21, Ephesians 4:31–32, and Colossians 3:8.* What is the source of rage and outbursts of temper? What should a believer's attitude be toward these emotions?

6. *Read Romans 6:11–18.* Substitute "anger" or "rage" every time the word "sin" appears. What has God done to free you from this sin? What must you do to experience this freedom?

## Chapter 9 ～∞～ Envy—The Green-Eyed Tyrant

1. *Read Genesis 29–30.* What do you think is the difference between jealousy and envy? Make two lists describing Rachel and Leah.

2. Remember that both Rachel and Leah had to cooperate in the wedding-night deception of Jacob. How do you think that affected Rachel and Leah's relationship with each other?

3. What did Rachel have that Leah wanted? What did Leah have that Rachel wanted? How did each woman try to get what she wanted?

4. *Read Genesis 31–32.* What was the sisters' attitude toward their father, Laban? What do we learn about Rachel in Genesis 31:33–35? What do we learn about her in 35:16–20?

5. Do you think either Rachel or Leah ever got over her envy of the other? What effect did their relationship have on their family life? On Jacob? *Read Genesis 37:1–11* and consider how their relationship continued to have an impact on their children, even after Rachel's death.

6. *Read Proverbs 14:30 and 27:4 and Song of Solomon 8:6.* In your own words write, what you think these passages' warn us about envy and jealousy.

7. *Read Mark 7:22, Romans 13:13, 1 Corinthians 3:3, 2 Corinthians 12:20, Galatians 5:20, and James 3:13–16.* How are envy and jealousy described in the New Testament? How do they affect us?

8. Do you feel jealous or envious of someone else for something he or she is or has? How has this affected your relationships and your spiritual life?

9. *First John 1:9* is the provision God has made to deliver you from destructive emotions, including envy and jealousy. Based on what you have learned, what will you do about it?

## Chapter 10 ∼∞∼ The Reality of Rejection

1. *Read Genesis 29:16–30:24.* How do you think Leah felt, knowing she was not as beautiful or as desired as Rachel? Imagine her feelings at Jacob's reaction when he saw who his bride actually was the next day. Do you think she felt rejection?

2. What do you think her marriage was like? Imagine the

different ways the statement "he loved Rachel more than Leah" was demonstrated in their marriage.

3. How did God compensate for Leah's rejection? In that day what gave a woman status and value?

4. What were Leah's expectations when she bore her first son? Were they fulfilled? What was she willing to settle for by the time she had her third son?

5. Where had Leah's focus shifted when her fourth son was born? What conclusion does it seem she arrived at?

6. *Genesis 30* records the mutual jealousy and competition between Rachel and Leah. What do we learn about Leah in what she named her maid's children? What does the incident with the mandrakes (which were thought to produce fertility) tell us about Rachel? Leah? Jacob?

7. *Read Genesis 33:1–3.* What did Leah want from her husband when her sixth son was born? What does Jacob's arrangement of his family indicate? Imagine how Leah felt with the constant evidence that she was not loved no matter what she did.

8. Have you experienced rejection by your family, husband, children, or friends? How have you responded? Has it diminished your sense of worth?

9. *Read Ephesians 1:3–14 and 1 John 4:7–19.* Write down all the things described in this passage showing what God did to demonstrate His love and acceptance of Leah. How might your feelings change if you base your value on God's acceptance rather than human rejection?

## Chapter 11 ～∞～ Greed: A Fearful Master

1. *Read 1 Kings 21.* Why did Ahab want Naboth's land? *Read Numbers 36:7 and Leviticus 25:23.* Why didn't Ahab

just appropriate it? What was his attitude when Naboth refused?

2. Why do you think Exodus 20:17 is included as one of the Ten Commandments? What can result from coveting? What were the results in the story of Naboth, Ahab, and Jezebel?

3. *Read Luke 12:13–21.* Meditate on Luke 12:15, substituting your own name for the word "man's." Then list all the things you consider valuable. Name each of these "valuable" possessions individually in place of the words "abundance of his possessions."

4. *Read Luke 12:21.* What do you think Jesus meant by the phrase "rich toward God"? How does a person become "rich toward God"?

5. Explain in your own words the meaning of *Luke 16:13.* Have you had an experience that proves the truth of this statement?

6. *Read 1 Timothy 6:6–10 and 17–19.* What are the dangers of wanting to "get rich"? How is the love of riches described in this Scripture? What is the warning in Proverbs 23:4–5?

7. What kind of wealth should we desire instead of material wealth? What is the difference between this kind of wealth and material wealth?

8. What things have you set your heart on—a better house, car, furniture, clothes? From a practical standpoint, how do you reflect an attitude of being "rich toward God"? In what practical ways are you laying up treasure in heaven? Do you need to confess the sin of greed and materialism and change the direction of your life?

## Chapter 12 ~∞~ Pride's Subtle Masks

1. *Read 2 Chronicles 26.* What were Uzziah's accomplishments? How do you think he felt when he saw enemies defeated and the country secure? What does 2 Chronicles 26:5 say was the reason for his success?

2. *Read 2 Chronicles 26:16.* What led to Uzziah's downfall? What did he do that was forbidden? What made him think he could do it? What were the consequences?

3. When you look at all the good things Uzziah did, why did this one act virtually end his effective reign? Can you think of reasons for God's severe judgment? What lesson can we learn from Uzziah's story?

4. *Read Deuteronomy 8:10–18.* What are the dangers we face when we experience success? What is the difference between pride and a sense of satisfaction?

5. *Read Proverbs 8:13; 11:2; 13:10; 16:5, 18; and 29:23.* What problems can pride cause us? What is God's view of this attitude?

6. *Read Psalm 31:23, 101:5, 138:6; Romans 12:16; 1 Corinthians 13:4; 2 Timothy 3:2; and James 4:6.* What else do we learn about pride in these verses?

7. *Read 2 Corinthians 5:12, 7:4, 8:24; Galatians 6:4; and James 1:9.* When is it all right to be proud? Is there someone about whom you feel this kind of pride? Write a principle about pride that you've learned from these passages.

8. What do you take pride in—your family background, home, income, appearance, accomplishments, social status? How has this affected your attitude toward others who are not in the same situation you are?

9. Select one of the verses cited in questions 5, 6, or 7 above that is most helpful to you and then memorize it.

Ask God to make it real in your life and to cleanse you from the sin of pride.

## Chapter 13 ~∞~ Inferiority—Another Form of Pride?

1. *Read Jeremiah 1.* What purpose did God have for Jeremiah's life? When did He make those plans? What light does this throw on the humanity of the pre-born child?

2. How did Jeremiah respond to this great responsibility? What emotions did he feel? Do you think he was justified in feeling this way?

3. What was Jeremiah's message to be? Would he be a popular preacher? What effect do you think this had on a person of Jeremiah's temperament?

4. What promises did the Lord make to Jeremiah? How did God equip him? How would Jeremiah be able to fulfill his ministry in the face of the opposition of the nation's leaders? What principle can we learn from Jeremiah's experience?

5. Is a feeling of inferiority or inadequacy an acceptable reason for refusing a responsibility that is offered to us? Have you ever done this?

6. *Read 2 Corinthians 2:16 and 3:4–6.* Did the apostle Paul always feel adequate for his tasks? What gave him confidence and ability?

7. Do you have feelings of inferiority and inadequacy? Do you have doubts about your ability to be a good mother? To keep your job? To get or keep a husband? To make good friends?

8. Where have your feelings of inferiority come from? What past experiences have reinforced them? What experiences have refuted them? Do you find it harder

to believe good things about yourself than negative things?

9. *Read John 15:5; Philippians 2:13, 4:13; and 2 Timothy 1:7.* In what specific areas do you feel inferior or inadequate? How will these verses help you overcome feelings of inferiority? How will you apply them?

## Chapter 14 ᴖ Dealing with Disappointment

1. *Read Exodus 2:11–15 and Acts 7:23–25.* What expectations did Moses have when he intervened to stop the Egyptian from beating the Hebrew slave? What emotions do you think he felt after his failure? What conclusions do you think he came to in his forty years of caring for sheep in the wilderness?

2. *Read Exodus 3:1–5:23.* What were Moses' expectations this time when he went back to intervene on behalf of the Hebrew captives? Why was he discouraged? *Read Exodus 6:1–10.* How did God encourage him? *Read Exodus 6:12.* What was Moses' response? What did that indicate?

3. *Read Numbers 11:1–25.* Why was Moses so discouraged this time? What did he ask for? In what two ways did God answer his request? What does this tell us about the methods God uses today to help us when we are overwhelmed?

4. *Read 1 Samuel 27:1–12.* What did David's discouragement cause him to do? What role did he have to play? *Read Psalm 7:1–2.* In what better way did he handle this problem another time? What principle in spiritual warfare do we learn from this incident?

5. *Read Luke 24:13–27.* What expectations did the disciples have? Were they right? What does Luke 24:21 describe as their reason for being disappointed? What are

some reasons for our disappointments today? What can disappointment lead to?

6. *Read Luke 18:25, 31–32.* Do you think Jesus was disappointed with the disciples? What should they have remembered? What did Jesus say would have cured their disappointment?

7. What failed expectations have you had? Have you responded with disappointment and discouragement? From your study, what have you learned is the cure for disappointment and discouragement? Will you do it?

## Chapter 15 ～∞～ Dwarfed by Discontentment

1. *Read Exodus 15:22–25, 16:1–16, and 17:1–7.* What was the reason for the Israelites' grumbling in each of the incidents described? Who did they grumble against? Who does Exodus 16:8 identify as their real target? What did the Lord do each time they complained? Why was He so patient with them?

2. *Read Numbers 11:1–35 and 14:1–45.* After two years, how did the Lord respond to the Israelites' constant complaining? Why was He angry? What should the Israelites have remembered? What severe punishment did He finally decree? What does this teach us?

3. *Read Numbers 20:2–13 and 21:4–8.* Did the people learn anything from their severe punishment? What further punishments did they bring upon themselves? How does this instruct us about God's attitude toward complaining?

4. *Read 1 Corinthians 10:1–13.* What are we supposed to learn from Israel's example? How does a complaining attitude harm us emotionally and spiritually?

5. *Read Philippians 4:11–13 and 1 Timothy 6:6–8.* What did

Paul say he had learned? Why do you think this has to be learned? What are our natural tendencies?

6. *Read Philippians 2:14, James 5:9, 1 Peter 4:9, and Hebrews 13:5.* What are we told to do without grumbling? Why should we be content? *Read Ephesians 5:20.* What is the antidote for complaining?

7. Is there something you often complain about? Even if you don't verbalize it, do you think it? Do you usually look for the flaw in everything? Is it difficult for you to enjoy life? Confess your discontent as sin. Memorize one of the verses cited in questions 4, 5, or 6 above and say it every time you are tempted to grumble.

## Chapter 16 ～∞～ The Agony of Grief

1. *Read Ruth 1.* What was the significance of Naomi's loss in that day? What positive and negative things do her instructions to her daughters-in-law reveal about her? What does Ruth's response tell us about her?

2. What was Naomi's emotional state on her return? Whom does she blame for her condition? Do you think this was justified? *See also 1 Kings 17:17–24.*

3. *Read Lamentations 3:32–39 and Psalm 119:67.* What are some of the reasons God allows us to suffer affliction and grief? What are the benefits?

4. *Read Ruth 2 and 3.* Read Ruth 2:19–23 and consider when Naomi's faith begin to revive. Trace how God worked behind the scenes in Naomi's life to keep His promise in Deuteronomy 10:18. What people did He use?

5. *Read Luke 7:11–15 and John 11:1–44.* How did Jesus respond to those who were grieving? What does this tell us about expressing genuine grief? What do we learn from

Him about helping others who have suffered loss? What insights do we learn from these passages about the attitude believers should have toward death? *See also Hebrews 2:14 and 1 Corinthians 15:51–57.*

6. *Read Psalm 10:14, 147:3 and 2 Corinthians 1:3–4, 7:6–7.* What do we learn from these passages about God as our Comforter? What methods does He use to comfort us? Can you think of times He has used these methods to comfort you? How does He use our sorrows to equip us to help others?

7. Have you suffered loss of some kind—a loved one's death, the end of a relationship, loss of property, moving away from friends, loss of health? What have you learned that can comfort you and strengthen your faith? What steps do you need to take when you are faced with sorrow and loss?

## Chapter 17 ～∞～ Lessons in Loneliness

1. *Read Jeremiah 1 and 2.* What indication do we have that Jeremiah would lead a very lonely life? Would he be a popular preacher?

2. *Read Jeremiah 16:1–8.* What else did God demand of Jeremiah that increased his loneliness? What was the basic reason for his isolation? What message did God intend that isolation to bring?

3. *Read Jeremiah 37 and 38.* Why was Jeremiah beaten and thrown into prison and into the cistern? How could he have prevented this abuse? Why didn't he? What means did God use to help him?

4. *Read Jeremiah 8:18–9:2, 15:10–18, and 20:7–18.* What emotions did Jeremiah experience and express? What did he accuse God of? How did he feel about the way people treated him? What did he wish for himself?

5. *Read Jeremiah 20:11–12; 31:31–34; 32:17–27, 37–41; and 33:1–9.* What did Jeremiah believe about God that comforted him in his suffering and loneliness? *Read Jeremiah 33:1–9.* What did God promise about Jeremiah's country that gave him hope?

6. *Read John 7:5; Mark 3:21; and Matthew 26:34–56, 27:46.* What different kinds of loneliness did Jesus experience? What was ultimately the worst abandonment of all? *Read 2 Corinthians 5:21 and Hebrews 3:18, 4:15–16* to learn some of the reasons for His suffering.

7. *Read Psalm 68:6, 27:10; Matthew 28:20b; and Hebrews 13:5–6.* Is loneliness always bad? What are good reasons for loneliness? What do we learn through loneliness to help ourselves and others? How does loneliness shift our dependence from people to God?

8. Do you ever feel lonely? Are you lonely for friends? For family? For a husband? In your marriage? Are you lonely for God? What steps of faith can you take from what you've learned in this study?

## Chapter 18 ∞ Friendship's Precious Gift

1. *Read 1 Samuel 14 and 17.* List the ways in which Jonathan and David were alike. How did they differ? What principles about friendship do we learn from these observations?

2. *Read 1 Samuel 18.* Who took the initiative in Jonathan and David's friendship? How might we have expected Jonathan to treat David in view of Jonathan's father's jealousy and fear of David's potential power? What does this tell us about Jonathan?

3. *Read 1 Samuel 19 and 20.* What did Jonathan do to protect David? How did this affect his relationship with his father?

4. What was the covenant Jonathan and David made with each other in 1 Samuel 20:13–17? *Read 1 Samuel 23:15–18.* How did Jonathan keep this covenant? *Read 2 Samuel 9.* How did David keep this covenant? What was the usual procedure when a new dynasty came into power?

5. *Read 1 Samuel 15:26–28.* What did Jonathan believe and accept? What does this tell us about Jonathan?

6. What does 1 Samuel 23:16 tell us about the spiritual dimension of Jonathan and David's friendship?

7. Describe the qualities of this friendship with specific adjectives. Do you have friendships with these qualities?

8. Is there someone you would like to have as a close friend? How might you initiate the friendship? What do you expect to get from it? What are you willing to give to maintain it?